MW00611027

"The remarkable thing about the truth is that it has an undeniable ring to it. That is the case with Ryan Haley's book, *A Better Way*, which resounds with biblical truths. Ryan's story was a page-turner and had me reading late into the night with the aim of ensuring I'm living out the principles he details in his book as he encourages us all to 'live a life that demands a supernatural explanation.'"

—JAMES BROWN, Network Broadcaster

"Ryan Haley has landed on a topic that is surely on God's agenda for today. His concept of *A Better Way* will surely lead you into what Jesus invites you into... 'Come to me, I will refresh your life.' (Matthew 11:28 TPT) This refreshing rest is what all of us need, it is what Jesus offers, and it is what *A Better Way* is all about. Ryan surely knows the value of strategy and the power of focus; but he has found something even better!"

—RICH MARSHALL, Author: *God@Work, God@Work II, God@Rest*

"*A Better Way* is an enlightening read full of practical and historically accurate investment information. A true testimony of how God's miraculous grace manifests in measurable ways! Business-minded individuals... do yourself a favor and read this book!"

—BILLY EPPERHART, Founder of Tricord Global and WealthBuilders, Inc.

"I am a believer in the power of a testimony to ignite change; those who want to experience God's absolute best in their business will be inspired both by Ryan's story and the Kingdom truths revealed in *A Better Way*."

—SHAE BYNES, Founder of Kingdom Driven Entrepreneur and Author of *Grace Over Grind: How Grace Will Take Your Business Where Grinding Can't*

"Ryan Haley is a man of authenticity who seeks to see people set free to walk in the fullness of all God has for them. With rare candor and directness, Ryan has penned a pathway for us all to access this fullness in our personal and business lives. In Ryan's own words, the following pages will offer you an invitation to '... trust God by making the counterintuitive and countercultural decision to give up your own human wisdom and strength in exchange for God's wisdom and strength.' Discovering God's best by investing your time in rest is a paradox that awaits you here. If you are prepared to accept the invitation, read on!"

—MARK APPLEYARD, Founder of Anothen

"It's a compelling read! It puts the teeth of testimony to increase the strength of my own beliefs. It is such a memorable read, you can actually talk to someone about it and share the author's discerning wisdom."

—BOB BOYLAN, Master Trainer to Fortune 500 companies, Author, and Photographer

"Ryan does a masterful job of bringing to life the book's central theme of God's grace and rest through the cessation of self-effort. By connecting personal testimonies and illustrations to the Word of God, he shows us how the supernatural meets the practical in life and business. As someone who deals with the complexities of leading a multi-congregational church and international ministry, I have been encouraged and inspired by the life-giving truths contained within these pages."

—PASTOR JEROME ("PJ") FERNANDO, Senior Overseeing Pastor, King's Revival Church, Sri Lanka and International Speaker and Author, Pastor Jerome Fernando Ministries

"I wish *A Better Way* had been written years ago as it would have saved me much toil, exhaustion, and pain. Ryan Haley has perfectly captured vital principles for doing business God's way, a way that leads us into the Sabbath Rest for the people of God. This book demonstrates the ease of Heaven as we partner with Him to fulfill our assignments. *A Better Way* is a must-read for every Kingdom-minded business leader!"

—JAMES KRAMER, Founder/CEO Commissioned and Pneuma33 Creative

"Ryan believes that God's supernatural grace and power will always eventually manifest in practical and measurable ways. And Ryan has lived in such a way that he can prove it. Revolutionary in approach, *A Better Way* is a tremendous resource. Ryan's writing is inspired, practical, and transforming. This book will help you discover that God is for you and how believing this changes everything. In Ryan's own words, 'By believing for God's best instead of following earthly wisdom, I am now not only debt-free but able to live entirely on passive income as a result of this property.' I believe this book will help you lay hold of peace and financial freedom."

—JASON CLARK, Author of *Prone To Love,*
God Is (Not) In Control, and *Untamed*

"I tend to believe the lie that my effort is necessary to accomplish God's plan. Ryan Haley's concept of a better way through exchanging our self-effort for God's wisdom and strength is such a great Kingdom principle that I intend to apply to my own life."

—MARTHA BRANGENBERG, Co-Host of The iWork4Him Show

"What a journey! Ryan delivers when he says he will show how the supernatural meets the practical. The story he shares in this book has many twists, turns, ups, and downs, but they always bring us back to the need to rest and relax and let God be God. Great job, Ryan."

"Sometimes God has to unravel the ridiculousness all around us: our schedules, our jobs, our places of residence, just to get our attention and to redirect us to his attention. As Ryan Haley says in his latest book, *A Better Way*, 'God was showing me in this season about the sacredness of rest as He went to work on my behalf.' If only as Christ followers we could learn this lesson the easy way. I laugh because God has me in exactly this position in my life right now. This book will inspire you, through Ryan's story, to look for God's hand in your life and respond with trust, waiting, and resting. This is a book for the ages, especially my ages!"

"I can highly recommend Ryan's book *A Better Way* to anyone who is involved in the marketplace. Ryan deals with a paradox that most entrepreneurs and business people struggle with. Surrounded by a world that promotes hard work and social media that screams daily 'only hard work will lead to success,' it is easy to misinterpret Jesus' promise: 'Truly, truly, I say to you, he who believes in Me, the works that I do, he will do also; and greater works than these he will do....' (John 14:12).

The word 'works' in the verse above is not about miracles and wonders. It is the Greek word *ergon*, which translates as 'an effort or an occupation.' The same Greek word is used in the verse: '...let your light shine before others, so that they may see your good works and give glory to your Father who is in heaven.' (Matt 5:16). The paradox is not in Jesus' promises. The paradox is how we can do 'greater works' to point others to the Father from a place of rest in a world obsessed by doing.

As a catalyst for change, I have seen many leaders reconnect to their source of life but not many renew their view of rest. Without this shift in thinking, the behavior of 'doing' does not change; therefore, neither does the outcome. In this book, Ryan shares his own journey of discovering what it truly means to live as a king in the Kingdom of Heaven. His authentic life story is a passionate invitation to invest in the best."

—ARJAN VISSER, Change Agent, Executive Coach,
and Facilitator at Business Revivalists

"I grew up in a family of hard workers and inherited a self-reliant philosophy that work is good and that one could have anything they wanted if they were willing to work hard enough to get it. Over time, two things have tempered that philosophy: 1. age, and 2. a holy ambition to go after the plans and purposes of God. His ways are higher than mine, so I quickly find I can't work hard enough on my own to achieve them. There must be a better way. That's the way Ryan unpacks in this book. Jump in, learn the way of rest, and trade your striving and stressing for God's strength."

—MICHAEL SIPE, Chairman, 10x Catalyst Groups and #1 Best Selling
Author of The AVADA Principle

GOD'S DESIGN *for*
LESS STRESS, MORE REST,
AND GREATER SUCCESS

A BETTER WAY

Living a Life that Demands a
Supernatural Explanation

RYAN HALEY

ISBN: 978-1-950710-30-0 (Amazon Print)
ISBN: 978-1-950710-31-7 (IngramSpark) PAPERBACK
ISBN: 978-1-950710-32-4 (IngramSpark) HARDCOVER
ISBN: 978-1-950710-33-1 (Smashwords)

For bulk purchase and for booking, contact:

Ryan Haley
https://ABetterWayPodcast.com
Ryan@GodsBetterWay.com

Because of the dynamic nature of the Internet, web addresses or links

contained in this book may have been changed since publication and

may no longer be valid. The content of this book and all expressed opinions are those of the author and do not reflect the publisher or the publishing team. The author is solely responsible for all content included herein.

Anonymity Note and Bible Versions:

For the most part, individual names of people I personally know have been changed to protect the privacy of those people mentioned. The names of public figures have not been changed.

All Scripture quotations marked (NIV) are taken from the Holy Bible, New International Version®. Copyright © 1973, 1978, 1984, 2011 by Biblica, Inc.™ Used by permission of Zondervan. All rights reserved worldwide. www.zondervan.com. The "NIV" and "New International Version" are trademarks registered in the United States Patent and Trademark Office by Biblica, Inc.™

Scripture quotations marked (TPT) are from The Passion Translation®. Copyright © 2017, 2018 by Passion & Fire Ministries, Inc. Used by permission. All rights reserved. ThePassionTranslation.com.

Scripture quotations marked (NKJV) are taken from the Holy Bible, New King James Version®. Copyright © 1982 by Thomas Nelson. Used by permission. All rights reserved.

Scripture quotations marked (NASB) taken from the New American Standard Bible®, Copyright © 1960, 1962, 1963, 1968, 1971, 1972, 1973, 1975, 1977, 1995 by The Lockman Foundation. Used by permission.

Scripture quotations marked (MSG) are taken from The Message Version®, Copyright © 1993, 2002, 2018 by Eugene H. Peterson. Used by permission of NavPress. All rights reserved. Represented by Tyndale House Publishers, a Division of Tyndale House Ministries.

Scripture quotations marked (AMP) are taken from the Amplified Bible Version®, Copyright © 1954, 1958, 1962, 1964, 1965, 1987 by The Lockman Foundation. Used by permission.

Scripture quotations marked (AMPC) are taken from the Amplified Classic Version®, Copyright © 1954, 1958, 1962, 1964, 1965, 1987 by The Lockman Foundation. Used by permission.

Scripture quotations marked (NET) are taken from the NET Bible®, Copyright © 1996–2016 by Biblical Studies Press, L.L.C. All rights reserved. Used by permission.

Scripture quotations marked (NLT) are taken from the Holy Bible, New Living Translation, Copyright © 1996, 2004, 2015 by Tyndale House Foundation. Used by permission of Tyndale House Publishers, a Division of Tyndale House Ministries. All rights reserved.

Scripture quotations marked (ISV) are taken from the Holy Bible: International Standard Version®, Copyright © 1996–forever by The ISV Foundation. All rights reserved internationally. Used by permission.

ACKNOWLEDGEMENTS

I'd like to personally acknowledge and give my sincere gratitude to a number of people who have made this book possible.

I want to start by thanking Jesus for His goodness, grace, and blessings that have saved and transformed my life. You are the inspiration for this book; I give You all the credit, glory, honor, and praise.

Secondly, I want to thank my mom, Rowanne Haley, for her tireless editing and feedback that stole her life for several weeks. More than that, you and Dad have been the best parents I could ask for, and I'm so grateful for your unconditional love and faithful support.

I want to thank someone who I've promised will remain anonymous but who has been one of the greatest sources of encouragement and blessing through their feedback, editing, and generous contribution to the book fundraiser. You have manifested the love and grace of God to me.

Mark Appleyard: I don't know if or when I would have written this book without your mentorship, coaching, wisdom, and encouragement. You embody God's love, integrity, and excellence.

Coach Tony Dungy: I am blessed and honored beyond words for your willingness to write the foreword. Above all, I want to thank you for your humility, authenticity, integrity, and impeccable example as a faithful man of God.

Everett and Ignite Press: Thank you so much for your expertise and professionalism!

I want to thank the following people for their endorsements of this book: James Brown, Rich Marshall, Shae Bynes, Billy Epperhart, Mark Appleyard, Bob Boylan, Pastor Jerome "PJ" Fernandez, James Kramer, Jason Clark, Jim and Martha Brangenberg, Tim Winders, Mike Sipe, and Arjan Visser.

Finally, I want to thank everyone who made this book possible through your generous donations to the book launch fundraiser: Oleg Sokolon, Sharlene Salvatierra, Larry Dowden, Nathaniel Spiers, Kelly Kolb, Rachelle Putt, Brandon Peery, Kevin Bohren, Melanie Burciaga, Jerry Prendergast, Lauren Jones, Bob Boylan, Tim Winders, Mark Appleyard, Steve Flores, Tristam Griffith, Sandra Spiering, Johnny and Jeanie Rhodes, Jeff Goers, Paige Haley, and Rowanne Haley.

To all my friends and family who weren't specifically mentioned, I want to thank you for being part of my journey with God bringing my dreams to reality.

TABLE OF CONTENTS

FOREWORD

I met Ryan Haley for the first time in 2018 at a Charis Bible College Men's Conference. As we got to know each other over the course of that weekend, I found Ryan to be a bright, energetic young man who had a vision for what he wanted to do with his life. He was involved in several projects at that time, but his overriding desire was to help people, and he really believed that God was preparing him to do just that. He felt that many of his life experiences, along with what he was learning in his college coursework, were giving him a unique perspective on life.

When I attended the conference again in 2019 and saw Ryan again, that vision had crystallized. He had found a formula for success in business and life, that he wanted to share with others. He was sure this formula would help people to maximize the assets and abilities God has given them and to find true success in their chosen careers. His blueprint was different than what is taught in most business schools or in the "School of Hard Knocks" that many of us have attended. But he was very confident in this plan because it's actually one that has proven to be successful over thousands of years and has a very solid foundation. The only problem is that it goes against conventional wisdom and the norms of today's culture.

As Ryan and I began to discuss his "better way" to business success, it intrigued me because I had gone against the grain in my career. I coached in the NFL for 28 years, from 1981 through 2008, and during that time was confronted with all the axioms that had been passed down in our business. Over the first 50 years of professional football, people had come to the conclusion that if you wanted to be successful, you had to work harder and longer than your competitors. You had to be more demanding and not show any sign of weakness. You had to give your players the impression you had prepared for every possible situation— that you were in complete control no matter what challenges confronted your team.

That sort of job description led many coaches I knew to work unbelievable hours and put their staffs through that same type of regimen. There were stories of coaches working 18-hour days, even sleeping in their offices many nights of the week so they could out-work and out-prepare their opponents. As some of these coaches became very successful, winning championships and Super Bowls, that formula came to be not only accepted but expected. Pushing yourself, your staff, and your players almost beyond physical limits became commonplace.

However, I was fortunate and blessed to play and coach for a man who didn't do things that way. Chuck Noll led the Steelers to four Super Bowl titles in the 1970s, but he believed there was more to life than just football. Having a quality family life, developing a purpose away from the game, and giving back to the community were things he valued above winning championships. He demonstrated this to us every day, and during the ten years I worked for him, I saw that you could be successful doing things in a way that might be different from most of your peers. Twenty years later, when I became head coach of the Tampa Bay Buccaneers, I followed Coach Noll's blueprint rather than the crowd.

In Ryan Haley's book, *A Better Way*, he lays out a way to be successful by actually doing less. It's a concept that doesn't sound logical. However, his premise is that knowing what you can do and what God expects you to do will allow you to have a better understanding of the things that you **don't** have to do. It's definitely a different concept. Most books on how to find success in the business world are going to give you a list of things you have to do in order to work your way to the top. But Ryan concentrates on biblical principles and encourages us to take advantage of the things God promises to do **for** us, so we don't try to do His job.

I have to warn you, the concepts Ryan lays out in this book are very simple to understand. However, they're not easy to follow. It will involve not trusting in our own intelligence and hard work, not following some time-honored principles of the business world, and most importantly, not following the crowd. For most of us, that is hard to do. But, just as Coach Noll showed me many years ago, sometimes there is a better way to approach things than the way everyone else is doing things.

If you're serious about pursuing success in business and in life but you want to follow biblical principles and do it the Lord's way, I would encourage you to read this book. I believe it will not only be challenging and thought provoking, but it will lead you to a great mission statement for your career. You'll be led to work hard, work with diligence and efficiency, but to ultimately rely on God and not on your efforts to make you successful. And this "better way" will free you up to enjoy life much more as you pursue that success.

TONY DUNGY

Joshua 1:8

THE BOTTOM LINE UP-FRONT

I want us to start with the end in mind and give the "bottom line, up-front" for you as the reader. So, to establish expectations before you start reading this book, I want to make clear what this book and its central message *is* and is *not*. Let me start by defining what I mean by A Better Way: God's Design for *Less* Stress, *More* Rest, and *Greater* Success.

Therefore, this is *not* another business or Christian book about "hard work." It is, in fact, about the **CESSATION OF SELF-EFFORT** and all of its associated and endless performance, striving, toil, stress, and anxiety. It is about unlocking the blessings of the Kingdom of Heaven by adopting the counterintuitively productive virtues of entering into God's **REST** and **EASE**, based purely on His incredible **Grace**. Many times, this flies directly in the face of our human logic, reason, and wisdom.

This is NOT a book about religion. We will most likely kill some sacred—as well as secular—cows here. Just like Jesus did in His day, I may shock and offend you at times, but that's OK because the true Gospel of Grace is SCANDALOUS to both the religious spirit as well as its counterpart, the self-focused flesh.

1

This *is* about **where the supernatural meets the practical** (as true spirituality *always* has a corresponding practical impact in the natural realm).

My goal is to demonstrate the intersection of Heaven and Earth. I generally find that at one extreme end of the spectrum, people are, as the saying goes, "so heavenly minded they're no earthly good'." At the extreme other end of that spectrum, many people give lip service to prayer and "faith" while operating exclusively from their own human abilities and getting hopelessly mired in the practical details and demands of business and life.

The purpose of *A Better Way* is twofold:

1. **Equipping:** Inspire by providing real-life examples to budding entrepreneurs and burned-out business owners in the household of faith that it is possible, and so much better, to walk by faith through Grace and do things God's way than to strive and toil in our own human effort and wisdom.

2. **Evangelistic:** Blow the minds of business-savvy people who don't yet have a personal relationship with Jesus with testimonies from real-life business owners that demand a supernatural explanation, which can only be explained through a relationship with Jesus!

The purpose of this book is to use real-life stories and testimonies as a vehicle to illuminate truths from the Word of God. My hope and belief is that this will encourage, inspire, and set you free with the "almost-too-good-to-be-true news" Gospel of God's Grace and Rest through the finished work of Jesus Christ. So here's the "bottom line, up-front:" it is my heartfelt desire and expectation that by reading this book, you will:

1. Have a life-changing revelation of God's goodness, nature and character

2. Have less stress, more rest, and greater success in your business and personal life

3. Depend more on God and less on yourself than you did before reading it

4. Be fully persuaded of—and personally experience—God's goodness in your businesses and personal life in practical, *measurable* ways

5. Trust God more and live less by sight and more by faith in practical ways

6. Be inspired and given permission to prosper greatly in your God-given purpose by tapping into your deepest passion, most natural strengths, and greatest contribution to the world

7. Have your own real-life testimonies to be a catalyst of helping others to achieve everything listed in numbers 1-6 above (in a nutshell, discipleship!).

As you read this, I trust and pray that the Holy Spirit will bring you into that Sabbath rest and ease God promises in His Word for New Covenant believers in Jesus. As you do, *please* share your testimonies and/or the testimonies of others you know so they can inspire and encourage others! You can submit nominations through *A Better Way*'s website at: https://abetterwaypodcast.com/nominations or send an email to me at Ryan@GodsBetterWay.com. I'd also like to encourage you to **sign up for *A Better Way*'s email update list,** which you can do at the bottom of the website homepage: https://abetterwaypodcast.com

I once heard a statement that I'll never forget: **"Our lives should *demand* a supernatural explanation."** That is what I hope this book will do: present testimonies and personal accounts that have Jesus as the only possible explanation, leading you into a deeper relationship with Him. I'd like to invite you into this journey of doing business and life *A Better Way.*

Grace & Rest,

RYAN HALEY

CHAPTER 1

CRASH AND BURN

I believe that hard work is ungodly.
I know, I know… I probably just dropped an incendiary grenade on many of you who are reading this, and you're probably shocked and offended by that statement. Fair enough. But before you put (or more likely, *throw*) this book down in outrage and call for me to be publicly stoned and crucified, please just hear me out first. I promise I will address this, both scripturally and experientially. First, though, I want to give you an overview of my background so you know where I came from and how I arrived at that belief.

Like many who are products of our driven American culture and predominantly legalistic Christian subculture, I grew up with a very high achievement and performance orientation. My mom once said that as a little kid, I would line up my shoes and toys in my room with military precision. I asked Jesus into my heart when I was about 8 years old at the Bible-believing, non-denominational Christian church I grew up in. From a young age, I had a desire to excel in school, sports, and a variety of extracurricular activities. For the most part, I did. I excelled academically, played a variety of sports, played trumpet in jazz band, was a member of National Honor Society, always kept my room clean, and eventually became an Eagle Scout.

By the time I got to high school, I had a pretty ingrained work ethic and high set of expectations for myself. Even though I was attending an academically rigorous college prep school and taking a number of challenging advanced classes, I would get extremely upset whenever I got that one B+ that got in the way of a perfect 4.0 (which somehow *always* happened!). I was never totally satisfied with my athletic performance, either, especially my cross country and track running times. I always felt like I could have pushed myself harder and gone a little faster—like I always had too much left in the tank at the end of the race.

This relentless, driven attitude seemed to lend itself perfectly to military service. I attended college on a Navy ROTC scholarship and was quickly indoctrinated into another level of Duty, Obligation, and Discipline (what I now refer to as the "DOD spirit").

This only increased as time went on, and I was commissioned as a Naval Officer upon graduating college. It ratcheted up another notch when I went to flight school as a student Naval Aviator, and then another after that once I had earned my "wings of gold" and reported to my first operational squadron as a warfare-qualified SH-60B "Seahawk" helicopter pilot (flying the Navy's maritime version of the Army's H-60 "Blackhawk" helicopter).

The issue at this point was that I was surrounded with many other driven, intelligent, high-performing people in an extremely performance-driven cultural atmosphere. Far from being consistently well above average compared to most of my peers, I was finding myself consistently *below* average and constantly feeling inadequate. I felt like I could never measure up to the standard of performance, behavior, professionalism, motivation, and execution that was expected and required.

Worse than all that, by this time I had strayed from my faith and relationship with Jesus. In order to distract myself from the gnawing sense that I was way off track with my life and my spiritual walk, I would spend most of my time zoning out with TV and blacking out with alcohol. At the time, I was deluded into thinking that I was having a good time and enjoying my life. After all, I was a "successful" young man enjoying the fruits of my labors from working hard most of my life to get to this point: I was a college graduate, a commissioned Naval Officer and helicopter pilot making good money, living in sunny southern California in a beautiful condo I owned, driving a sporty BMW M3, and partying with my old college friends now that I was back in San Diego. From an external perspective, it probably looked to most people like I had it made and was living the dream. But deep down inside, I knew I was becoming more and more empty and dissatisfied.

This all came to a head one afternoon. It was July 31, 2007. I remember that date because it's my dad's birthday, and it was about a month before my first scheduled overseas deployment. I was on a routine training flight conducting a practice maneuver called an autorotation in which we simulate engine failure and attempt to land without power. This is a fairly dynamic maneuver but one that I had performed hundreds of times before during training. However, on one particular attempt this day, I got significantly off safe parameters. My airspeed was too slow, and as a result, my rate of descent was too high. Instead of "waving off" and going around the runway pattern for another pass, I attempted to salvage a bad situation.

In doing so, I made it worse. *Much* worse. At an altitude of about 100 feet, the other pilot and I both realized something was seriously wrong and we both pulled full power. Unfortunately, by that point, it was too late to stop our precipitous descent, and we hit the ground... *hard*. So hard that the right main landing gear wheel broke off and hydraulic fluid sprayed my right-side windshield. Innumerable klaxons, warning lights, and cockpit indicators screamed at me, confirming what I already knew: I had just messed up—big-time.

Miraculously, we all walked away from the crash after recovering control of the aircraft and eventually making a safe landing back at home base. I say "miraculously" for good reason. I was told after the accident by the ranking officer of the safety mishap investigation board that he had run the models and simulations "seven ways from Sunday" and couldn't figure out how we survived. Based on data from the onboard computers that recorded the crash, the simulation showed us getting into a state called "dynamic rollover" in which the rotor's blades hit the runway and the aircraft violently rolls over on top of its occupants. Suffice it to say, that's a pretty bad day in a Naval Aviator's line of work and not something one typically walks away from.

Despite that, the other pilot and I escaped with very minor injuries. The aircrewman in the back had some back and neck injuries, but they were much less severe than they could have been. Just prior to the mishap, his safety harness had been unlocked. Even though the procedure calls for everyone's harness to be locked before entering the autorotation, in practice, many times the aircrewman will leave it unlocked for greater ease of movement around the cabin, which was the case in this instance. However, just prior to entering the auto, for no apparent reason, he providentially felt an urge to lock his harness, which most likely saved him from much worse injuries than he actually sustained.

Though we were all in much better shape than anyone could have hoped or expected, it was going to be a very long night of exhaustive medical tests, drug and alcohol screenings. Following that, there was an even longer period of shame and rumination on what had just been my single greatest failure in life. To add insult to injury, after the crash, I found out that debris from the very sophisticated—and *expensive*—electronic and flight equipment from this $30 million weapon system was strewn all over the runway.

This earned me the nickname—or "call sign" in Naval Aviation parlance—"Yardsale:" a reference to the kind of epic skiing wipeout wherein one leaves one's skis, poles, gloves, goggles, and other gear strewn several hundred feet down the mountainside. Despite perceptions propagated by movies like *Top Gun*, call signs are rarely, if ever, complimentary. Quite the opposite, in fact; they're usually meant as a form of humiliation to the recipient and derived from ignominious body parts, sexual references, and/or a humiliating incident. Embarrassing call signs or nicknames are like quicksand: the more you struggle against them, the deeper you go and the more you get stuck in it. My recommendation: Just give up the fight and maintain whatever dignity you have left at that point.

Worse than my newfound call sign, however, was the Navy's eventual decision that my flying days were over. I would no longer be in a flight status; I was permanently grounded. I felt like I had just crashed and burned my entire life. All those years of hoping and dreaming of being a Navy pilot, long hours studying in flight school, the blood, sweat, and tears I had put in to **earn** my wings, all seemed to amount to nothing but a painful reminder of my life's greatest failure. This was unquestionably the lowest point of my life. I was face to face with shock, disappointment, failure, and shame because of that failure.

I now believe that a critical part of the reason I had such a deep sense of failure and resultant shame is tied to putting my identity in my performance. I purposefully emphasized the word **earn** in the last paragraph. If everything of value comes to us because we earn it by our performance and self-effort, then those same things of value can just as easily be taken from us when our performance and efforts are unsatisfactory. To modify an old saying: "*Live* by performance, *die* by performance." To be fair, I will be the first to admit that it is absolutely staggering what human beings can accomplish solely from their performance, even apart from a relationship with God. That's because we are all creators, made in the image of our Creator.

However, even though it may not be as dramatic as a helicopter crash, at some point, we all crash and burn if we're living by self-effort and our performance. It may be your marriage, your health, your

"Live by performance, die by performance."

job, your finances, or any number of things. I once heard Bill Johnson (one-time Senior Pastor of Bethel Church in Redding, CA) say something that arrested me and has rung true: "Whatever is initiated by human effort must be *sustained* by human effort." Therefore, no matter how hard-working, smart, strong, disciplined, or otherwise good you are as a person, if you're living from your own strength and wisdom, it's not a matter of if—but *when*—the bottom falls out under you, just like it did for me in that Navy helicopter. That's the bad news.

But there's good news. In fact, it's nearly *too* good to be true...

PERSONAL REFLECTION AND PRACTICAL APPLICATION

Learn from my mistake! <u>Don't</u> <u>wait</u> until you crash and burn something in your own life to get right with yourself and with God. Take honest inventory of who and where you are, and ask yourself if this is who you want to be and where you want to be going. Whether it's your marriage and family, career, health, personal habits, or anything else, be willing to ask the hard questions and surround yourself with people who can help you in that process. If you already have crashed and burned, just know that God is with you and for you and can turn any setback into a setup if you'll rest in His grace and perfect love for you. Cry out to Him *now*; don't wait any longer!

CHAPTER 2

THE PRODIGAL
SON RETURNS

When it comes to doing business and life, God has a *better* way. We don't have to rely on and be limited by our own human abilities. As discussed in the last chapter, that sets us up for certain eventual failure in some area of our life and establishes a pattern where it's "*live* by performance, *die* by performance." And at some point, our own strength and abilities *will* let us down. With the Gospel of Grace, our pattern is "live under Grace, die to self."

I know that "dying to ourselves" may sound painful and sacrificial (and many well-meaning people in church and ministry certainly do paint that picture), but when I got a revelation of God's incredible Grace, I realized it is actually incredibly *liberating*. On my own personal journey of discovery, I've realized that to live under God's Grace and die to myself means I'm no longer judged or rewarded according to *my* effort, work, and performance. I get to live a life of

God has a better way. We don't have to rely on and be limited by our own human abilities.

13

blessing based on the *perfect* performance and *finished* work of Jesus.

As I mentioned in the last chapter, when I was working and flying at my operational Navy helicopter squadron, I never felt like I was living up to the high standards of performance and conduct that were expected of me. I constantly felt inadequate, guilty, and condemned because I didn't have a good enough attitude, enough motivation, and there was always something I wasn't doing well enough. Even though I had gone through the training and qualifications—and had my wings to prove it—I somehow never felt like I could do or be good enough.

Unfortunately, I believe most Christians feel the same way in their relationships with God. I know I did in my own Christian walk for many years. I knew of all the Bible stories and miraculous things God did in and through the heroes of the faith but somehow never experienced that same level of supernatural power in my own life, especially the ability to live free from sin and condemnation. Because I was born again and had the Holy Spirit inside me, I had *knowledge* of good and evil and felt genuine spiritual conviction about right and wrong. I even genuinely *wanted* to do the right thing (most of the time) but just didn't seem to consistently have the *power* to do so.

The Apostle Paul talked about this, too: "For we *know* that the Law is spiritual, but I am of flesh... not practicing what I would like to do, but I am doing the very thing I hate... for the *willing* is present in me, but the *doing* of the good is not. For the good that I want, I do not do, but I practice the very evil that I do not want" (Romans 7:14-15; 18-19 MSG, emphasis own). Even though I may not have been consciously aware of all this at the time, it resulted in a sense of frustration, exhaustion, and failure, which is why the allure and temptations of the world became so appealing to me.

14

After working so hard for so long both spiritually and practically, by the time I entered college, I was ready to just "coast" and ride the coattails of my hard work and success in life up to that point. I decided that it was time that I just relax and enjoy myself in this new phase of life. I started to "party hearty" at the beginning of my freshman year, developing a habit and reputation of consistent, heavy drinking until I blacked out (which would unfortunately last for about the next eight years until and even after my crash). Once I had secured the ROTC scholarship for the next three years of school at the end of my first semester, I even started doing drugs despite the fact that it could get me kicked out of ROTC and school.

Thus began a long, slow drift from God. I basically kicked him out of the Captain's seat of the aircraft in mid-flight, made myself the Pilot in Command, and departed the runway pattern He had me in. I set out on my own new proverbial course, heading and glide slope for a long time that very easily could—and by all rights *should*—have made me a literal smoking hole in the ground. But for God's Grace and (I believe) supernatural protection, that's exactly where I would've ended up. But not just from the helicopter crash. There were literally hundreds of times before (and even some after) the crash that I was driving drunk, which could and should have resulted in the same fate or multiple DUIs at the very least. I was consistently making irresponsible, reckless, and destructive decisions that very well could have cost the lives of many others in addition to my own.

I was in willful rebellion, consistently making choices I at some level *knew* could have seriously negative consequences but went right on sinning anyway. I honestly have no idea why I was spared disaster so many times and even escaped *unscathed* from numerous potentially life-altering or life-ending decisions and circumstances. What I can tell you for sure is that it had absolutely *nothing* to do with my goodness or righteousness. In

2015, I would get a profound revelation of how God's grace through Jesus' finished work operates with our faith and belief. But this was 2007 at the time, and I was reprobate and clueless, so this truly was **100% God's Grace** and **0% me or even my faith**. Looking back at things now, I clearly see all this as an amazing demonstration of God's Grace, or "unmerited favor," in my life.

This ties back to the earlier point about living under Grace and dying to self, which means *I* get to benefit from the fact that *Jesus* lived up to the perfect standard of the Law. It's something I never could, never can, and never will be able to do on my own merits. That is why it had to be Jesus as the perfect sacrifice to do it on our behalf. I've always lived my Christian life knowing that there was no way I could ever earn my eternal salvation apart from simple faith and trust in Jesus as my Savior. When it comes to

"Where sin abounds, grace abounds all the more."

this life, though, until relatively recently I thought and acted as if my success and God's ability to bless me was entirely dependant on *me*. By and large, I think many Christians are caught in this deception at some point in their walk of faith. As I've grown deeper and closer in my relationship with God, though, I've noticed more and more how amazing things happen that I had nothing to do with and don't deserve.

Case in point: in most instances, crashing a helicopter and being permanently removed from flight status is not exactly a career-enhancing move for a Naval Aviator. If anything, that kind of maneuver will more than likely get you a set of "hardship orders," the equivalent of moving to the back side of Midian and tending sheep like Moses did after he crashed and burned by killing the Egyptian. In any case, it is a virtual certainty that it won't set one up for a highly competitive, "sweet-deal" set of follow-up orders. Yet that is *exactly* what happened to me after crashing the helicopter. And it was 100% a result of God's Grace and unmerited favor. Paul says that "where sin abounds, grace abounds all the *more*." Some translations use the term "super-abounding favor," meaning that Grace not only gets you out of the hole, it actually sets you up even *higher* than you were before.

If you *allow* it, failure can actually be like a divine trampoline: The *lower* you go, the *higher* you go. Failure and sin can actually catapult you to greater success than you had before, where the set*back* becomes the set*up* for promotion. Again, I didn't get a full revelation of God's Grace until 2015, and at this point, it was 2008. What I *did* have an awareness of at that time was the fact that this failure was a wakeup call and an opportunity for a major life change.

As I said before, despite outward appearances, I knew deep down that my life was not going in a good course and heading. I had been subconsciously sweeping the conviction of the still, small voice of the Holy Spirit under the rug for years and trying to ignore His subtle but insistent impressions by distracting myself with TV, alcohol, friends, etc. This helicopter wasn't going to fit under the rug, though; it was too big. And praise God for it, because I needed a shock to the system, kind of like a defibrillator for someone whose heart has stopped beating: "*CLEAR!*" It's sad to admit, but this is how bad and how extreme it had to get for me to come to my spiritual senses.

There's actually a story in the Bible about this same thing, though, so I guess God knew it would happen often enough that He'd need to have an illustration for people like me to relate to. Most of you have heard of it: the story of the prodigal son (found in Luke 15:11–32). Like me, this guy had had enough of living under his Father's authority and covering and had departed the pattern to pursue his own course and heading in pursuit of his own desire to party hearty. And like me, this nearly made him a smoking hole in the ground as well.

After he'd squandered all of his inheritance on wild living in a different runway pattern, it got so bad that he found himself homeless and starving. He was so hungry and desperate that pig slop was looking quite appetizing to him. This was when he finally came to his spiritual senses.

And like me, when he finally did turn back to the arms of his loving father, not only was he not reprimanded, punished, or humiliated with a set of "hardship orders" as the hired help on the estate, he was actually given even *more* than he had before. In fact, his father was waiting for him from far off and *ran* to embrace and kiss him before he could even get his whole spiel out about what a terrible son he was, how badly he screwed up, and that he didn't deserve to even be called his father's son anymore.

God's grace can cause sin and failure to be like a trampoline, catapulting you into greater success.

Completely ignoring this (very true) confession from his son, the father *proceeds* to have his servants prepare a huge party for this recently reprobate younger son with the best food available. He even goes a step further by actually putting him in a place of honor and authority with the nicest clothes and his very own signet ring. Since he had already received his portion of the inheritance previously, this represented a "double portion." These are all extras and upgrades the son got, simply from returning to his father's house after doing nothing but willfully, enthusiastically sinning for an extended period of time. Hallelujah, I can relate!

This is a scriptural confirmation of what I mentioned earlier from my personal experience: *If* you *allow* it, God's grace can cause sin and failure to be like a trampoline, catapulting you into greater success. So, *how* exactly does one "allow" this to happen?

18

Just like the prodigal son in the biblical account, I had to come to a place where I was unflinchingly honest with myself about where I was, where I was headed, and who I was becoming. I had to admit that I did not like what I saw and that charting my own course and heading had taken me to a really bad place, and I needed to quickly adjust course and get back on glide slope ASAP.

In essence, I needed to *repent.* In fact, I *wanted* to repent, because I saw what a mess I had made of my own flight plan when I was the Pilot in Command. I wanted to invite God back into the cockpit, initiate a positive three-way change of controls to make sure He had *His* hands on the stick to control the aircraft, slide back into the left-side co-pilot seat, and let *Him* take over again. Again, contrary to popular opinion and religious tradition, "repent" does *not* necessarily mean to beat your breast, put on sackcloth and ashes, flagellate yourself, and feel horrible for what a rotten sinner and terrible person you are. It is from the Greek word *metanoia* and simply means "to change one's mind." In my case, I needed to change my mind about several things:

"Repent" does not necessarily mean to beat your breast, put on sackcloth and ashes, flagellate yourself, and feel horrible for what a rotten sinner and terrible person you are. It is from the Greek word metanoia and simply means "to change one's mind."

1) How fit I was to determine the direction of my own life

2) How "enjoyable" living a party lifestyle was, but most importantly,

3) What kind of Person my heavenly Father was and what living in His house *actually* looked like.

Like the prodigal son, I had a misperception of the nature and character of both my Father as well as life on His estate. Many times, I thought of Father as a harsh taskmaster and of life on His estate as drudgery, obligation, and inferior to the pleasure I could find out in the world. I needed to see my Father and my situation clearly in light of the truth. He loves me infinitely and unconditionally for who I am, no matter what I did or how badly I screwed up. I had to *repent* about just how good He was and how badly He wants to shower me with blessings, even and especially when I *least* deserve them. This is so we can be crystal clear on the fact that our blessings from God are in no way dependent on, or the result of, us and our efforts. It is exclusively the result of His goodness, love, mercy, and grace.

In fact, the Bible says that it's actually the *goodness* of God that leads people to repentance. For a long time, I thought it was His judgment and wrath that brought people to their knees in fear, shame, and repentance. Human nature being what it is, many times, that is the way things unfold, but that is *not* God's preferred way to reconnect with us; He just uses whatever we give Him. Like any truly good Father, He would much prefer to lavish us with blessings and favor to convince us of His nature and everlasting love for us and His sincere desire to be in relationship with us.

This was something *else* I needed to repent of! My mind just couldn't believe that He could possibly be this *good*. I've heard it said that the traditional translation of the Gospel as "Good News" is

> *It's actually the goodness of God that leads people to repentance.*

inaccurate in that it's too understated and not sufficiently emphatic. Supposedly, a more accurate translation would be something to the effect of "the *too*-good-to-be-*true* news!"

I was starting to get a taste of this after the helicopter crash. Once I had recognized in no uncertain terms how far off course I was, I repented and came back to my Father's house. It was on my birthday, September 8, 2007. I got down on my knees with my parents on a family vacation in Mexico and humbly asked God to come back into the right-side seat and take the lead for the flight. I was sufficiently tired and broken in spirit from living life my way to surrender my life back to Him for His good purposes. Again, though, I want to be clear that it's not *God* who beats us into submission to coerce us back into obedience as some would portray it.

Unlike the Old Covenant, in the New Covenant, God doesn't have us on a short leash and *never* teaches us lessons by bringing hardship or failure upon us. In reality, God allows us what seems to be almost an irresponsible amount of freedom in our choices. When doing things our own way inevitably brings us to our knees, it's not *Him* that brought destruction and calamity down on us. It's our own decisions and the natural law of sowing and reaping that gets us to those places where we're exhausted and broken, finally desperate enough to come back to God when we can't take it anymore.

That being said, God can and will use *all* things in a pattern for our own good (Romans 8:28). This many times includes—but is certainly *not* limited to—our own unwise, destructive, or otherwise poor decisions and lifestyle choices: sin, failure, disappointment, etc. Human nature being what it is, many if not most of us *do* learn the hard way. But, to borrow a real estate term, it's not God's "highest and best" for us to get bailed out from a crisis or desperate situation by a miracle, like my helicopter crew and I did in the crash.

There's a better way. That is to remain in God's Grace and rest so that blessings can actually seek us out and overtake us.

Once again, there's a *better* way. That is to *remain* in God's Grace and rest so that blessings can actually seek us out and *overtake* us. This is what happened to me after the helicopter crash with that unbelievable set of follow-on orders I mentioned earlier. But before I go into that, I want to briefly provide you more context. There were some things that led up to that divine trampoline bouncing me higher in life and blessings overtaking me that I think are important to discuss.

Once I had repented and rededicated my life to God, I started going to church and got involved in fellowship outside of just attending church services. I started to address my excessive drinking and began to exercise and eat healthier food than I had before. I was gradually becoming a healthier person overall. This was all the natural outflow of a deep and sincere repentance of the heart. I believe that a sincere repentance (which is simply "changing of one's mind") always eventually has visible fruit. But before the fruit can be seen, the root must be dealt with.

In order for repentance to take place, I believe one must be in a place where they are *willing* to change their thinking, and consequently, their behavior. I believe repentance requires a humble heart, a teachable spirit, and an open mind to see, accept, and receive new possibilities. It requires a *personal choice* to allow hardship, failure, difficulty, challenges, and/or setbacks to make one *better* instead of bitter and to *expect* "goodness and mercy to follow us all the days of our lives" (Psalm 23:6). It also always eventually requires a willingness to give up control and trust God with outcomes, even and especially when it means giving up something precious to us. This was a lesson I would soon learn in a very real way.

PERSONAL REFLECTION AND PRACTICAL APPLICATION

Have you been steering your own heading in life that has taken you down a dark road? Are you off course? "Repent" (change your thinking) of your own human strength and wisdom, and start depending on God's grace (divine empowerment) to help you in every area of your life. Return to your loving Father's house of blessing and abundance. Let Him wrap you up in His love and help you turn your life around. Humble yourself and give Him the controls to get you to a far better destination. He's not going to condemn or crush you, no matter what you've done. He's waiting for you to return to Him so He can restore and bless you!

CHAPTER 3

FROM SETBACK TO SETUP

My Commanding Officer (CO), Commander (CDR) Crain called me into his office one day and asked me a question that caught me off-guard. He asked me to seriously consider whether or not I felt I *should* continue as a pilot, whether or not I thought I *could*. He said he clearly saw that I was motivated and willing to do whatever it took if I could and that this was a difficult thing to consider, but that he wanted me to do so very objectively. He suggested I take some time off and get out of my current environment to be able to remove myself to sufficiently ponder this decision.

He then asked me if there was any way I could get away and go spend some time with my family or some people close to me to really think about this. That was a miracle in itself, because I was scheduled the next week or so to go to Cancun, Mexico, for my birthday and visit my family on what was originally supposed to be pre-deployment leave. After the crash, though, I was scheduled at the same time to see Commander, Naval Air Forces (or CNAF, the three-star Admiral who is in charge of all of Naval Aviation) as part of the evaluation board following the aircraft mishap. I was really disappointed that I was going to have to cancel this vacation I was really looking forward to and in many ways needed.

Even though he technically did not have the authority to do so, CDR Crain said that as my CO, he was going to grant me six days of leave so that I could go down to Mexico with my family and seriously consider this (I'd later learn that instances like this where people make exceptions to policy for my good are hallmark characteristics of God's favor). Surprised, with a full and grateful heart, I went to Mexico. It was down there, on my birthday, that I got on my knees, repented, and prayed for God to come back into my life, as I mentioned earlier.

After praying and pondering CDR Crain's question to me for that week with my parents, I felt I was sensing the Holy Spirit leading me to the conclusion that I did not have the wisdom, experience, or judgment required to make such a decision and that I should trust whatever decision CDR Crain's wisdom and experience led him to. I told him this when I got back. He made the decision that I would continue flying in a probationary syllabus with careful observation, which if I completed successfully, put me back into an operational flight status and a deployment shortly thereafter.

The first few flights were really rough, and Murphy's Law was in full effect. We had maintenance malfunctions, in-flight emergencies, weather issues, and runway patterns I had never before seen because of unprecedented wind patterns. It threw me off my game pretty badly, in addition to the fact that I was already rusty from having been out of the cockpit during the investigation board for many months by this point. I figured for sure that if they were going to pull the cord on me, it would've been at this time. However, somehow, I made it through those first several difficult flights, and eventually, I felt like I had some momentum going for me.

On my last flight, I actually caught a radio call nobody else did, which was great because my biggest weakness had been identified as my situational awareness (SA, for short). When I went home that night, I started going through a Bible workbook that challenged the reader to pray about one or several things every single day for a specified amount of time until I clearly heard God say one of three things: yes, no, or wait. The number one thing on my list that night was whether or not I could and would continue as a pilot. I had no idea how long I would be in prayer for that answer to come, but I was committed to consistently and faithfully praying until it did. When I went to bed that night, I had a dream that CDR Crain called me into his office and told me that I would no longer be flying. This made no sense to me whatsoever based on the previous day's flight and my demonstration of an ability to overcome a major weakness.

I woke up from the dream, wrote in my journal about it, and then when into work. Lo and behold, CDR Crain called me into his office and told me that I would no longer be flying based on what seemed like a very minor issue in the previous

God had so clearly spoken to me...it gave me a total sense of peace and encouragement.

flight. Just like in the dream, it made absolutely no sense to me whatsoever, and it certainly was not at all what I was expecting or hoping for. But the fact that, in response to my prayer the night before, God had so *clearly* spoken to me through a supernatural gift of the Holy Spirit (in what I would later find out is called a "prophetic dream"), it gave me a total sense of peace and encouragement; just as *all* spiritual gifts—and especially the gift of prophecy—are designed to do (1 Corinthians 12 and 14). This was a perfect real-life example of the what the apostle Paul talks about in Philippians 4:6-7 (NIV):

Do not be anxious about anything, but in every situation, by prayer and petition, with thanksgiving, present your requests to God. And the peace of God, which transcends all understanding, will guard your hearts and your minds in Christ Jesus.

After CDR Crain had made his decision, I saw the Wing Commander, who was the next level up in the chain of command regarding my flight status final decision. He seemed shocked by CDR Crain's decision, and asked me if I agreed with it and was willing to accept it. It really seemed like he was willing to go to bat for me if I decided I wanted to continue flying. But I told him what I told CDR Crain: I had prayed and felt that God told me to defer to whatever decision CDR Crain made and that I was willing to accept full ownership of that decision with total peace. He silently shook his head in bewilderment as he signed the papers that would eventually permanently remove me from flight status.

Even though it went against the grain for me at the time, I felt a sense of peace and relief that I couldn't quite explain. I think this circumstance gave me a permission I didn't even know I needed to let go of my striving as an operational pilot and step into a new season. Even though this decision should've caused me confusion, frustration, anger, and bitterness, by surrendering to what I felt was the still, small voice of the Holy Spirit as well as submitting to the God-given authority over me (CDR Crain), I was able to attain a sense of peace and resolution. In response to prayer, I had been sincerely willing to sacrifice my flying career on the altar, and when it was indeed taken away from me, I was pleasantly surprised with how I was able to maintain such a sense of settled peace, assurance, and even relief. This is an example of living under God's Grace and dying to self. And God's grace actually made it *easy* for me to do!

I do not believe God was "sovereignly" controlling events such as the crash, my response to it, or CDR Crain's decision that I wouldn't fly anymore. As mentioned before, I certainly do not believe He was the Author of all these things. I *do* believe He was able to *use* it in order to facilitate change for my good. But I had to be *willing* and *available* to submit to those changes. In Matthew 23:12, Jesus says, "He who humbles himself will be exalted, and he who exalts himself will be humbled." Therefore, I believe humility is a critical ingredient in being able to benefit from the divine trampoline. Luckily for me, that was pretty easy at this point in my life since I had no pride left to speak of. Adversity and failure have a certain way of making you humble.

This is an example of living under God's Grace and dying to self. And God's grace actually made it easy for me to do!

But again, that is a choice one gets to make. It *was* possible that I could have allowed the crash and CDR Crain's subsequent decision to make me prideful, bitter, and even worse off than I was before. Even though I was spiritually comatose for those many reprobate years, I do believe the Holy Spirit was working on me all the while on the inside, so that when the opportunity presented itself, the pump had already been primed inside me for a willing, cooperative change. So for that, I credit God's Grace once again for setting me up for success in the midst of failure.

After I was taken off flight status, I initially did *not* get a dream set of orders. In fact, I got a 12-month set of orders to Iraq as part of what was called an Individual Augmentation (IA). IA was a program the military had at the time in which the Navy was trying to do its share to help out an overextended Army in the midst of a protracted insurgency in a landlocked theater as part of the war on terror in Iraq and Afghanistan. Navy personnel were embedded with an Army unit, wearing an Army uniform, doing an Army job. At this point in the war, Improvised Explosive Devices (IEDs), or roadside bombs, were killing a lot of Coalition Forces. My particular set of orders involved working in a Counter-IED unit to stop this threat.

You have to understand that to a Navy helicopter pilot flying out of beautiful San Diego, this set of non-flying orders in the desert with the Army truly was the real-life, modern equivalent of toiling in obscurity on the backside of the desert in Midian. But the squadron in San Diego had become a toxic place for me, a daily reminder of my shame and failure, and a place that no longer had any purpose or opportunity for me. In short, I was ready to get out of there as soon as I possibly could, and this was a welcome chance to make a fresh start. So I was ready to go and actually excited for what God had in store for the next chapter of my life. I enthusiastically filled out all the pre-deployment paperwork, got all the medical tests and pre-deployment screenings, and had plans in place to rent out my condo to a tenant while I was gone.

With just two weeks before I was scheduled to leave, I was already halfway packed and out the door, eager for what the Lord had for me next and ready to be on my way. It was then that the Executive Officer (XO, or second-in-command at the squadron) casually remarked as he passed me in the hallway: "Hey, you heard your orders got cancelled, right?" I should have been overjoyed, but mentally I was already on my way "downrange" (an informal military term used to refer to being in a combat zone), so this really threw me for a loop. I had done all the necessary preparation to head out and would have a tenant shortly renting out my condo. What would I do next? How long would I have to carry my shame at the squadron? Where would I live?

I asked the XO for more details, but all he could say was, "I don't know; orders for both you and your alternate just got cancelled without explanation; this came from the top." Indeed, I believe it most certainly did come from *the* Top— the Commander-in-Chief of Heaven's Armies! I now believe that because I had maintained a humble heart, a teachable spirit, and an open mind for new possibilities, God was setting me up on His trampoline. As I was praying and talking about this with the Lord, I sort of got the sense that (to a *very* small degree) I was experiencing the blessing of Abraham, who was willing to make a tremendous sacrifice of what was most dear to him in life and trust God for the outcome. I had put my wings on the altar, been willing to walk away from flying, and I was willing to make that sacrifice no matter where it took me, even if that meant the deserts of Iraq. Little did I know that, just like He did with Abraham, God was about to send me my ram in the thicket...

After the IA got cancelled, I needed a new set of orders. After working with my "Detailer" (the Navy's term for the person who identifies and coordinates your next set of military orders) for a week or two and not finding anything very exciting, one day she called me with a very interesting and unexpected opportunity. Apparently, her cubicle was right across from the Graduate Education Detailer, and due to a last-minute dropout she had a "billet" (another military term for orders, position, or "seat") that had opened up at the Naval Postgraduate School (NPS) in Monterey, California, in their business school for a Master of Business Administration (MBA) degree in Financial Management. They really needed to fill it ASAP. The only catch was that it was a "short-fuse" set of orders, and I needed to be there in two weeks.

At first, I dismissed the idea out of hand. Apparently not having completely learned my lesson from the botched autorotation, I was still trying to salvage my military career. I wanted a set of orders that would make me competitive for promotion. This was also when the Navy had just opened up a brand-new career path for Warfare-Qualified officers (which I was as a winged aviator) to do a lateral transfer to the new Foreign Area Officer (FAO) Corps.

This career track is basically the Navy version of the State Department's Foreign Service Officer (FSO) job. It entailed getting a Political-Military graduate degree, in-depth language training, and being stationed overseas as a Defense Attaché at an embassy or consulate. It also involves some level of intelligence-gathering. As someone who loves travel, foreign languages, and the idea of a glamorous job in Europe engaging in high-level diplomatic dinner parties and functions with dignitaries sprinkled with an element of intrigue, I was very interested in pursuing that option. Also, back then, I had no interest whatsoever in business, and it seemed like the timeline was too tight to make it happen.

I put the MBA option out of my mind for a few days and was catching up with my mom on a Friday. She asked how the search for orders was going, so I filled her in on the Monterey orders for the MBA. As I heard the words coming out of my mouth, I started to realize what a great opportunity it was. So did my mom. She incredulously asked me if she had heard correctly that I had been offered the opportunity to go to beautiful Monterey, CA, where I *wouldn't* be shot at and taking incoming mortars, to get *paid* to earn my MBA on the Navy's dime with full active-duty pay and benefits, *and that I had turned the offer down?!* Well, when she put it like that, I guess it did seem pretty stupid...

My mom encouraged me to talk to a man named Captain (CAPT) Silver, who was a mentor. He had been my Commanding Officer (CO) during my formative military training days in ROTC at the University of San Diego. He had had a long and

32

distinguished naval career as the CO of a ship, and had retired at the rank of a "full bird" (O-6, or Captain). He embodied the values of Naval service to me, and I just assumed he would encourage me to do whatever it took to get back on track in the Navy. When I met to talk with him on Monday, I was very surprised that he said nothing of the sort.

In fact, what he said was that this MBA option was a tremendous opportunity for me and not to worry about trying to salvage my career. At this point, he said, I needed to do what was right for *me* and simply accept the gift that life (God) was trying to give me. This completely shocked me, but it also freed me up not to make a decision based on obligation or what I felt I "should do" (back to that old DOD spirit) but didn't really want to.

The truth was that I actually didn't even really *want* to make a career out of the Navy; I just felt like that was "what you do" as someone in my position. I didn't really consider what I *wanted* to do, and this gave me the freedom to do that. This is a real-life example of what it means to "die to self." It means dying to self-effort, striving, toil, and our own ability. In this instance for me, it meant letting go of the false obligation (that wasn't even mine to begin with!) to be a "Due Course Officer" and salvage my career and simply accept the incredibly good gift my good Father was extending to me. This version of "dying to self" was *much* easier than what I had been led to believe for most of my life. This was a transition from living and dying by my performance to living under Grace and dying to self.

> *"Dying to self"...was a transition from living and dying by my performance to living under Grace.*

It also gave me a renewed perspective about God. I was worried that this deal was "too good to be true" (which I *now* know is literally the essence of the Gospel of Grace) and that maybe the enemy was trying to trick me with this "bait." What God told me during this time was, "Just because something is a really good deal, Ryan, doesn't mean it's not from Me. Sometimes, I *like* to give you really good deals." Again, I was having to *repent* and think differently about the nature of God and what He wants for me.

Since then, I've even had to repent about repentance, personal sacrifice, and death to self. God's Grace even makes it easy for us to repent, sacrifice our ways and plans, and die to ourselves so we can live *from* Christ! Notice I did *not* say, "*for* Christ" but rather "*from* Christ." That's because He Himself is the One who is at work within us to place the very longings and *desires* to work for His good pleasure! That'll get you out of the DOD spirit! As you'll read later, this is a lesson I have had to learn over and over again and am *still* learning. God will let us go around the mountain as many times as it takes for us to learn the lesson He's trying to teach us. Thank God that He's longsuffering and patient with us as we go through the process. What I've found is that most times the lesson I need to learn is not to keep underestimating His goodness and the pure joy of the **very good** plans He has for me.

> *God will let us go around the mountain as many times as it takes for us to learn the lesson He's trying to teach us.*

After this conversation with CAPT Silver, my mom all but *ordered* me to email the Detailer first thing Tuesday morning and *beg* to accept those orders if they were even still available. I agreed. As it turned out, I didn't even need to. At the very top of my email list was a note from my Detailer with the subject line "Monterey." In the email, she strongly urged me to reconsider taking the orders to Monterey. I immediately responded to say I was sold and just needed to know what to do next to make it happen. As it turned out, all I needed to do was have my undergraduate transcript from the University of San Diego faxed over to NPS in Monterey and fill out some basic paperwork.

This in itself is another amazing testimony of God's unmerited favor over my life. First of all, these sets of orders to Monterey—and especially the MBA program—are extremely competitive and hard to come by, even for what we call "Due Course" Officers (meaning highly competitive, upwardly mobile career Officers being groomed for promotion to command). Additionally, there is usually a fairly rigorous and involved application process, which in many cases, involves taking the Graduate Readiness Exam (GRE) or a similar test. For a non-competitive Officer who had just crashed an aircraft and wasn't even in a flight status and therefore no longer a member of the "tip of the spear," to get these orders without having to do anything more than fax over my undergraduate transcript (which itself was not very impressive) was nothing less than an act of Divine Providence.

But it doesn't end there. Originally, I was not going to be able to attend my childhood friend's wedding and be his best man because I would be in Iraq. As a result of the order change, I was able to be there for one of my best friends on one of his most special days as his best man. Also, because I had recently prepared to leave for Iraq and rented out my house, I was in a position where I actually *could* make it on that tight timeline after all. Additionally, I *already* had a corporate renter lined up to rent out my condo.

Because of a housing shortage in San Diego and huge demand at the time in the corporate rental space for one-bedroom units, they would be paying me **$1,800/month** (in

2008 dollars) for my one-bedroom, one-bathroom, 729-square-foot condo conversion. This was beyond anything I could reasonably expect and something I hadn't even considered initially, and it made a huge difference later. This is because rent in Monterey was *not* cheap, and we would be experiencing a once-in-a-generation financial crisis. Two weeks later, I had left the squadron and was attending grad school in Monterey.

I had done absolutely nothing of my own merit to earn any of it, other than crash a $30 million helicopter.

Last, but certainly not least: I couldn't possibly know this until several years later, but this new set of orders qualified me for eligibility in a program that would later be created and known as the Housing Assistance Program (HAP). HAP was designed as a government-subsidized financial assistance program for military members who had both bought homes and been forced to move *out* of those homes as a result of military orders (within a specified timeframe) during the financial crisis. The program stipulated that, for eligible candidates only, the military would cover the loss on whatever the subsequent sale of the home was.

Four years later, this would end up allowing me to prepare for military separation by selling my condo in San Diego at a 50% loss and help me walk away free and clear from it because of *$135,000* in military financial assistance. God had already made provision with the supply before I was ever even aware of the need! This was my ram in the thicket, my double portion, and my overtaking blessing. And I had done absolutely *nothing* of my own merit to earn *any* of it, other than crash a $30 million helicopter.

I couldn't even make this stuff up if I *tried*. God truly gives us superabundant grace in our time of need, even and *especially* when we don't deserve it. We can choose to live and die by our own performance and merits or *choose* to live under *His* Grace and unmerited favor as we die to our own self-effort, human wisdom, strength, and plans. As a result, we can enter into *His* plans for us (which are *much* better than ours) and the blessing and favor that *Jesus* deserves but earned *for* us. **We can have *our* way or a *better* way.**

PERSONAL REFLECTION AND PRACTICAL APPLICATION

Ask God how you can go "from setback to setup." Ask the Holy Spirit to give you a humble, teachable heart that will allow you to learn from your mistakes while not being condemned and held bondage by them. God's grace *superabounds*, or exceeds, your sin and failure. Be willing to let go of things you may be holding too tightly. I'm living proof He can turn things around and cause even your mistakes to prosper you. *Expect* amazing turnarounds to come!

CHAPTER 4

BAPTIZED AND SENT
TO THE DESERT

Not surprisingly, my time in Monterey was a great season of life and helped me get that fresh start I had been hoping for when I was in the squadron. I did really well in school, graduating from my MBA program with a 3.9 GPA, and really enjoyed being back in a scholastic atmosphere. I got plugged in with a great Bible study men's group at school and a good church group, so I grew a lot spiritually. With the addition of healthy eating, regular exercise, fresh ocean air, and a beautiful area to live in, I had a newfound zest for life that was good for the mind, body, and spirit.

I was still really interested in becoming a Navy FAO and even tried to transfer over to the Political-Military degree at NPS, but I was told in no uncertain terms that I had been billeted, and was most definitely going to stay in, the MBA/Financial Management program. This was OK with me, though, since I knew that degree was probably one of the more broadly applicable and practically useful masters degrees to have. I even had a kernel of awareness and knowledge that, simply by virtue of how it was dropped in my lap, God must certainly have some kind of Kingdom purpose and plan for me with business, even though I still wasn't intrinsically interested or passionate about it at the time.

I developed some close friendships during the 18 months I was there and am still in touch today with some of my friends I met there. I also finally committed to complete and total sobriety from drinking at the end of my tour and started attending a Christ-centered 12-step group called Celebrate Recovery. That was another point of repentance that took me a while to get to. I knew I drank excessively and that it was a pattern, and therefore, a problem in my life. I just didn't think I was "one of those" who needed to attend 12-step meetings and make this whole huge deal out of it. I justified myself because I would go several months without drinking, was generally high-functioning, I was on a good track in life now, and for the most part, I only drank on the weekends with my friends. I knew how to keep my priorities in order, and that was generally evident in my life.

But the night before Thanksgiving in 2009, I went out with some friends and really tied one on to the point that I completely blacked out for a good six hours or more. Luckily, my friends took care of me, and nothing bad happened other than getting embarrassingly incoherent and inebriated. But it really scared me that I couldn't remember anything at all for a large portion of the night, and unfortunately, this was not by any means the first time that had happened. I realized that although I may not have fit the mold of the "gutter drunk" whose life was a complete disaster, with my all-or-nothing mentality and lack of an "off-switch" when it came to drinking, all it would take was one bad night or decision to make it so.

I got sober in Celebrate Recovery and maintained complete sobriety for about five years, with one fairly dramatic but (again, by God's grace) ultimately harmless exception. After graduating and leaving Monterey in December 2009, my next set of orders was further north up the West Coast in Bremerton, Washington, aboard the John C. Stennis (CVN-74, a Nimitz-class aircraft carrier). Ironically, this would actually be my first experience being stationed on a ship out at sea, even though I had been on active-duty Naval service for about seven years by that point.

Before I went there, though, I had to make a pit stop at a middle-of-nowhere little town called Dahlgren, in Virginia. I went to Dahlgren for six weeks of training in preparation for my role as a Tactical Action Officer (TAO) on the Stennis. The TAO is in charge of ship self-defense systems in case of an attack. This is a fairly weighty responsibility because a fully qualified TAO has weapons release authority from the ship's Captain to launch shipboard self-defense missiles and the Close-In Weapons System gun. This is basically a Gatling, or minigun, that can fire up to 5,000 rounds per *minute*.

There was nothing to do in Dahlgren but study and work out, so over that six-week time period, I took my exercise and health game to another level. I finished my tactical training in Dahlgren but kept my physical training going strong, as I once again moved back across the country to Bremerton, where it would go to yet another level. As I mentioned before, I sometimes tend to have a kind of extreme, all-or-nothing approach to things in life. Since I had stopped drinking completely now, I just switched that same intensity over to working out and healthy eating. Although right now it's not quite as intense as it was at that time, this habit pattern has generally stayed with me since then, for which I'm generally happy.

I also applied that same intensity and focus to my spiritual walk. I was really hungry and had a desire to go deeper with God than I ever had before. As I had gotten used to doing from all the moving around in the Navy, I quickly got plugged into a local church and played drums for the worship band (as I had in

Monterey as well). I also got involved in a home fellowship small group with some guys from the ship. This was a new level of discipleship and intentionality for me, so I was growing quickly. Analogous to my body's, my "spiritual metabolism" was getting into a peak state with a fire inside that was burning ever hotter.

Because Bremerton is only about three hours from my hometown of Portland, Oregon, I was able to go home on weekends fairly regularly. One weekend when I was back, my mom invited me to go to a church none of us had ever been to. They were having a conference that weekend with a visiting missionary minister who was also billed as a "prophetess." My mom had gone with a friend who had invited her the previous night and was intrigued by the different ways they worshipped and how the Holy Spirit moved in that place. I didn't have language for it at the time, but this was a charismatic church denomination that believes and operates in the modern-day supernatural gifts of the Holy Spirit. I know there is a lot of debate on this topic within the Church, but I encourage you to read the following section with an open mind and heart.

All my life up until this point, I had gone to what I would've called at the time a "regular"/mainstream kind of nondenominational evangelical church, which believes in the Bible and a relationship with Jesus but does not necessarily acknowledge or experience the supernatural power of God as depicted in the first-century New Testament churches of Acts and all throughout the Bible. Like my mom, I was unsure of what all this was, but I was intrigued and hungry for more of God, so I decided to go with her. On the way out of the house, my dad jokingly made a comment to watch out for the "holy laughter" that some people supposedly experience at these kind of tent revival-type meetings. I somewhat derisively laughed about it with an image of a healing televangelist "miracle worker" that steals people's money based on an elaborate showcase of parlor tricks, a là Steve Martin's character in the movie *Leap of Faith* (if you're familiar with the movie; if not, it's actually a pretty good one I'd recommend).

When my mom and I got to the service, the first thing I noticed that was markedly different than what I was used to was the fervent, free, and spontaneous nature of the musical worship. I was used to a pretty formulaic three-song worship component of the service before the pastor would give his sermon. But these people really seemed to be listening to and following the leading of the Holy Spirit to direct where *He* wanted to take the congregation, sometimes stopping and "camping out" on a single verse in the lyrics for several minutes at a time, as something seemingly important but as yet unknown to me appeared to be unfolding that was important for God to demonstrate. Another huge difference I noticed was that people were extremely animated and lively in their worship, throwing themselves into it with reckless abandon. Some of them were waving flags, some were moving around out of their seats, while yet others were doing funny-looking dances. All in all, I found it unusual, but because of my deepening hunger for the things of God, I was appreciative for the clear enthusiasm of the people in attendance.

After about an hour or so of worship, which was way longer than I had ever experienced before at church, the guest speaker finally came on and started her message. To be honest, I don't really remember most of what she said, but I do remember her talking about a powerful encounter she had when God clearly called her to "the nations" (whatever that meant). This encounter occurred within a very vivid dream that was unlike anything I had ever heard of or experienced, almost like the way I imagined dreams in the Bible to be for the likes of Pharaoh, Nebuchadnezzar, Solomon, the Old Testament prophets, or Joseph (the father of Jesus). The other thing I remember being struck by was this woman's absolute conviction and clarity in her calling and her unwavering belief that she had heard clearly and supernaturally from God about it.

At the conclusion of her message, she began to go up to individual people in the crowd and tell them something she felt God was telling her to say to them. I was struck by the specificity and what appeared to be depth of insight she had for people she had never even met before. Sometimes, it would be in the form of pictures; other times, it would be a description of something going on in somebody's heart or circumstances in their life, but apparently, this was the "prophecy" part of the conference I had heard and been intrigued about. After this went on for a while, she said she was going to move into prayer for each system of the body to be healed.

She then invited people to come up to the front of the sanctuary to receive prayer for healing if they wanted it. I was definitely expectant and hopeful for some kind of major breakthrough, but I didn't really feel like I needed healing in my body, especially with my now well-established lifestyle of extreme health and fitness. I was standing in the back, but for some reason, I shot up like a rocket to the front and center row on the left side of the room. Normally, I wouldn't do something like that, especially in a church I had never been to with people I had never met, but again, I was at a point of deep hunger and desire for more of God in this season of my life. I almost had the sense that I was like the woman with the issue of blood who had such a hunger to be touched by God that she was undeterred in moving close enough to Jesus just so she could touch the hem of His garment to be healed.

Once I was up front, if my memory serves me, the minister prayed systematically, starting at the feet and methodically working her way up according to the location and system of the body. She seemed to fully expect that people were going to be healed right then and there as she did this. Eventually, she got to the heart, and she even specifically asked people to raise their hand if they were dealing with high blood pressure. Many years before when I was in flight school, I was diagnosed with "essential hypertension" (high blood pressure primarily as the result of hereditary/genetic factors) and had been taking medication for years to mitigate it. I actually had to get a medical waiver in order to be aeromedically cleared for flight status.

However, as a result of my new and improved lifestyle, I had lost between 30 and 40 pounds since then and was in the best shape of my life, so I was no longer taking the medication. I still did technically have the prescription and the diagnosis, though, and hadn't specifically checked my blood pressure for a while, though

I felt what I can only describe as an electric current go from her hand into my chest and throughout my body.

I was pretty sure it was not an issue anymore. Either way, I kind of reluctantly raised my hand just for the heck of it, but almost out of a sense of obedience to some degree, since she had prayed for the heart and then got even more specific with the word about high blood pressure. I was definitely looking forward to some kind of "inner" or soul-level, versus physical, breakthrough with God, but I couldn't quite place my finger on what that was. So I just figured, "What's the harm? It can't hurt, right?"

Being that I was literally right in front of her, having come up from the back several minutes before, when I raised my hand, she stepped forward and laid her hands on my chest as she prayed for high blood pressure to be removed from my body. As soon as she did, I felt what I can only describe as an electric current go from her hand into my chest and throughout my body. I had never experienced anything like this before, so I was

45

surprised and taken aback. She noticed this and asked if this was my first time receiving prayer like this, which I confirmed. She asked again if she could put her hands on me and continue praying for me. I said yes, and once again, as she put her hand on my chest right where my heart was, I felt that same electrical current. It was not painful like an electric shock, but it was definitely noticeable as a physical sensation in my body.

Then it happened...for no apparent reason, I started to laugh. Much to my horror, the laughter kept increasing in intensity as she kept praying for me with her hand on my chest. I was embarrassed at first because I had no idea *why* I was laughing, and other than my mom, I was surrounded by a bunch of people I had never met before. I almost had the sensation that I was watching myself laugh as a neutral third-party observer. After another five to ten seconds or so of this though, I decided I was not going to fight it anymore and just fully submitted to it. I began laughing *uncontrollably*, just as my dad had mentioned before I left the house, and ended up falling backward on the ground and was promptly covered by a purple blanket (standard charismatic fare, as I would later discover).

I continued laughing on the floor long after she had moved on to pray for someone else. As I did, I had the sensations of what I can best describe as bubble wrap being popped inside each cell of my body. I know that probably sounds weird, but I can assure you it was an amazing feeling. A sense of warmth, joy, peace, and release seemed to permeate my entire being. I don't know if it was then or later that the Holy Spirit brought to my remembrance what Proverbs 17:22 says: "Laughter is good medicine for the heart."

Indeed it is, because several months later I would have my blood pressure medically and scientifically checked over a period of five days, multiple times a day by an Army doctor, who would confirm that I no longer had hypertension. Again, to be fair, I do believe that my drastic lifestyle changes account for a large part of this, but I also believe that God moved in a supernatural and unexpected way to heal me and give me a powerful demonstration that He was more tangibly real than I had ever experienced before.

I really didn't know what to do with this because it wasn't even on my grid, but I could not deny the experience I had just had. After the service, the friend of my mom who had told us about the conference gave me a CD by a pastor named Bill Johnson called *The Supernatural Power of a Transformed Mind*. In this multi-CD set, he proceeded to describe scripturally, as well as with one incredible testimony after another, how the supernatural power of the Kingdom of God that I was used to relegating solely to "Bible times" is just as powerful and real today as it was when Jesus or any of the other biblical characters walked the earth. I almost couldn't even believe my ears because it was inconceivable for me to think of that, having grown up my whole life as a Christian in church, I had never directly seen this or even really heard about it from anyone else. I figured that if this were real, I surely would have heard about it by now, right?!?

The more I dug into this and found more resources on it, the more I realized these kinds of things had been and were happening for many years but that I just hadn't been aware of or exposed to it. Scales started to fall from my eyes as Bill Johnson used scriptures I had heard and read literally hundreds, if not thousands, of times (like the Lord's Prayer) and skipped right over without even understanding or acknowledging. I now knew what Jesus meant when he said in Matthew 13:11–17 (TPT):

> You've been given the intimate experience of insight into the hidden truths and mysteries of the realm of heaven's kingdom, but they have not. For everyone who listens with an open heart will receive progressively more revelation until he has more than enough. But those who don't listen

with an open, teachable heart, even the understanding that they think they have will be taken from them. That's why I teach the people using parables, because they think they're looking for truth, yet because their hearts are unteachable, they never discover it. Although they will listen to me, they never fully perceive the message I speak. The prophecy of Isaiah describes them perfectly:

Although they listen carefully to everything I speak they don't understand a thing I say. They look and pretend to see, but the eyes of their hearts are closed. Their minds are dull and slow to perceive, their ears are plugged and are hard of hearing, and they have deliberately shut their eyes to the truth. Otherwise they would open their eyes to see, and open their ears to hear, and open their minds to understand. Then they would turn to me and let me instantly heal them.

But your eyes are privileged, for they see. Delighted are your ears, for they are open to hear all these things. Many prophets and godly people in times past yearned to see these days of miracles that you've been favored to see. They would have given everything to hear the revelation you've been favored to hear. Yet they didn't get to see as much as a glimpse or hear even a whisper.

Could it possibly be that I had been one of those people who hadn't had an open, teachable heart and therefore could not receive the revelation and experience the supernatural power of God's Kingdom in this current age of empiricism and science? Was it possible that now I had become soft and open-hearted enough to perceive and experience what so many had yearned for so long to see? Was this level of access, power, and insight into the reality of the Heaven's Kingdom possible, for *me,* to actually *see* the supernatural in this day and age?! According to Jesus' very own words once again in John 14:11–12 (TPT):

Believe that I live as one with my Father and that my Father lives as one with me—or at least, believe because of the mighty miracles I have done. I will tell you this timeless truth: the person who follows me in faith, believing in me, will do the same mighty miracles that I do—even greater miracles than these because I go to be with my Father!

It all just seemed too insane, fantastical, and ridiculous to be true, yet as someone who had always thought and said that what was in the Bible was true, I could no longer deny the clear and obvious words I was reading, especially in combination with the physical experience I had just undergone that served as mutual confirmation. I felt like a kid in a candy store, and I tried to get my hands on and eat as much as I possibly could of this new flavor of Christianity.

As it turned out, I wouldn't have much time to dig into that just yet because the IA orders to Iraq that were suddenly and unexpectedly cancelled in 2008 had come back around to me, this time to Afghanistan. Within a month of this experience, I had orders to deploy, and following two months of stateside training, I was deployed and embedded with the US Army in Afghanistan by August 2010. As a friend of mine would later insightfully observe: Like Jesus, I had been baptized in the Holy Spirit and shortly thereafter sent to the desert for testing.

PERSONAL REFLECTION AND PRACTICAL APPLICATION

Ask the Holy Spirit to gently (or powerfully) show you if there is some aspect of truth in the Word of God that you currently may be unaware of or close-minded about. This could be about the supernatural gifts of the Holy Spirit, God's unconditional love and grace, a specific situation or relationship, etc. Ask your Heavenly Father if there is a blessing He wants to give you that you're not receiving for whatever reason. There's always more of God to be discovered and tapped into!

CHAPTER 5

GOD QUALIFIES
THE UNQUALIFIED

My combat orders to Afghanistan were a part of the troop "surge" in 2010 to 2011. This Afghanistan troop surge, as part of Operation Enduring Freedom, was inspired by the success of the first surge the US instituted in Iraq. I was part of an all-Navy group that would be embedded with an Army unit once in-theater. This command was called Tactical Document and Media Exploitation-Afghanistan (TACDOMEX-A, or DOMEX).

As its name suggests, the DOMEX mission was to exploit documents and media such as cell phones and computers for informational value. DOMEX teams supported the Intelligence ("intel", or S2) branches of the Army and Marines by providing this information for their analysis in order to identify and target enemy networks. The other aspect of the mission was to provide prosecution value to law enforcement professionals to put bad guys in jail.

Originally, I was stationed at one of the main bases in Afghanistan called Bagram Air Field. As far as Afghanistan bases go, this one afforded a good quality of life because of all the amenities it had. This was a small city that had thousands of people in it, the majority of which, surprisingly, were civilians. I was the deputy (meaning the assistant, or #2 guy) to the Division-level DOMEX officer for that region. We had a fairly robust team of five or six people at a time, depending on transient personnel movements to and from the base as they were traveling to other parts of the country for their assignments.

As a fairly senior Lieutenant, I probably should have been the overall Officer-in-Charge (OIC) of my own DOMEX unit on a smaller base, but during the two months of stateside training we did as a unit before we got downrange, I tended to be generally "behind the curve" and easily overwhelmed by tactical situations. As a result, when the teams were being assembled by the ranking officers of our unit, they decided it would be best for me to be under the guidance and support of a senior officer. Some people may have been offended by this, but to be completely honest, I was perfectly OK with it since I didn't want the stress and pressure of being responsible for my own team, and I was happy with being on a big base with good quality of life.

Part of that is because I had never been operationally deployed before, spending all of my time in the Navy either in a training status or at grad school. As of yet, I had no actual combat leadership experience. Not only that, but DOMEX was a totally unfamiliar discipline to me in an unfamiliar Army environment and culture. We were wearing Army uniforms, but as Navy guys, we were still the proverbial stepchildren of whatever Army unit we were part of. And then, of course, there was the fact that we were in an active combat zone as part of a ground unit. All of those things combined to make me feel out of my element, isolated, and overwhelmed.

Within the first week or so of getting to Bagram, I started to feel the anxiety building. I didn't feel confident in my ability to do the job. As the days wore on, I became increasingly anxious, overwhelmed, and frustrated with my seeming inability to become proficient at my job and settle into a stable rhythm. I was praying and reading the Word a lot, crying out to God for help and perspective to deal with the inexplicable anxiety I was experiencing but couldn't seem to get out of the hamster wheel that was constantly turning in my head. One of the things that served as an escape for me was my daily two to three-hour exercise regimen at the gym to get the blood flowing and the endorphins pumping through my body. But even that was marginally helpful against the flood of cortisol relentlessly coursing through my veins.

In retrospect, I believe a large part of it was that my immediate superior had a fairly hands-off leadership style and gave me a lot of latitude. Also, we took different shifts so we were frequently not in the workspace at the same time. A lot of people may have liked this and done well in that environment. But when learning a new task in an unfamiliar context, I personally don't do well with ambiguity. I prefer specific and frequent feedback, guidance, and direction. I also have a tendency to make mountains out of molehills and be my own worst critic by putting more pressure on myself than anyone else would. So, a lot of this was a mental prison of my own making. But whether or not this pressure and stress I was feeling was objectively rèal or just in my head, it was all too real to me.

Despite my inner turmoil at this time, somebody saw something in me that no one else did. In this case, that somebody was Lieutenant Colonel (LTC) Cooper, Director of TACDOMEX-A. She was always making her rounds to the various bases scattered throughout the country under her command (a great example of the business management principle "management by walking around"). After spending some time with my team and observing me when she came to Bagram, she decided that "LT Haley needs a team of his own, and we need a new location." While I appreciated her confidence in me and the fact that I'm sure in her mind she was doing me a huge favor, I wanted nothing to do with it. I was under enough stress and had enough problems just dealing with where I was in a relatively ideal environment. I had no interest whatsoever in going to a brand-new location in a very "kinetic" (Army terminology for "dangerous and violent") geographical area of the battlefield and having to stand up a team from scratch.

However, that is precisely what happened. I was sent from Bagram to a little town called Andar, in the Ghazni province. Andar was located approximately halfway between the capital city of Kabul and the major southern city of Kandahar. It was a hotbed of insurgent activity because of the supply and logistics routes the Taliban and other insurgent factions were using to transport weapons, communications, and other supplies. This Forward Operating Base (FOB) had just been established about a month prior to my arrival, which meant that services and amenities were very limited.

We had only a few small decontamination showers, very limited running water, and no flushing toilets for the first six months. My Navy brethren and I had to actually build our own tent when we got there. Suffice it to say, this combat deployment with the Army had definitely become my "Navy appreciation tour." It definitely gave me a greater sense of respect and appreciation for what the Army "grunts" have to go through on their deployments.

My "client" (the Army unit I was supporting with TACDOMEX capabilities) was an Infantry Battalion: the storied 101st Airborne Division. I was having to learn a whole new set of acronyms, terms, and nuances of the Army's highly centralized hierarchy and command structure. These guys were a different breed, for sure. Army infantry units in general are a pretty rough-and-tumble bunch of characters, but these guys were especially gruff because they were already 10 months into a 12+ month deployment. They had maintained an almost superhuman operational tempo and had not appeared to be slowing down at all for the last two months.

If anything, they seemed to be increasing their operational tempo. Despite that, these guys were clearly living up to their historic reputation as seasoned and effective combat professionals who knew how to get the job done and were clearly putting a serious hurting on the local insurgents who up until recently had been operating with total impunity in this area. This unit was definitely a model example of a well-oiled combat machine.

God...doesn't always pick the people who appear to be the most obvious choice, the best and brightest, who are the most qualified for His assignments.

When I first arrived at FOB Andar, I only had one other person on my team, Operations Specialist Second-Class Petty Officer (OS2) Hawkins. I had worked with OS2 Hawkins during our stateside training as well as at Bagram. I appreciated his work ethic, dependability, and straightforward, common-sense approach to getting the job done (which I sometimes lacked when I got way too cerebral in how to think about structuring and organizing a task). LTC Cooper had offered me the pick of the litter when it came to who my enlisted subordinate would be and was surprised when I chose Hawkins.

I feel like this is a picture of how God works many times: He doesn't always pick the people who appear to be the most obvious choice, the best and brightest, who are the most qualified for His assignments. As the saying goes, "God does not call the qualified; He qualifies the called." In fact, the Bible consistently shows a pattern of God doing almost the total opposite. The Apostle Paul discusses this in 1 Corinthians 1:26-30 (NKJV):

For you see your calling, brethren, that not many wise according to the flesh, not many mighty, not many noble, are called. God is using the foolish things of the world to put to shame the wise, and God's chosen the weak things of the world to put to shame the things which are mighty, and the base things of the world and the things which are despised God has chosen, and the things which are not, to bring to nothing the things that are, that no flesh should glory in His presence. But of him you are in Christ Jesus, who became for us wisdom from God—in righteousness and sanctification and redemption—that, as it is written, 'He who glories, let him glory in the Lord.'

To be fair, OS2 Hawkins was nowhere near as unqualified as the above passage of scripture depicts. Objectively, I would say that I was actually a much less likely candidate for my position than OS2 Hawkins was for his. God doesn't make mistakes when He chooses seemingly unqualified candidates for His assignments who, somehow, despite themselves and their own inabilities and weaknesses, are able to get impossible results with His Grace and empowerment. Similarly, by the end of this deployment, it would become abundantly obvious to everyone in TACDOMEX that neither LTC Cooper nor myself had made such a personnel mistake either, despite our seemingly foolish personnel selection criteria for assignments. This certainly came as a huge surprise to everyone, most of all me.

This is because of a truth that has become so clear and powerful to me over the last several years, and is one of the major themes of my podcast (also called *A Better Way*): "The foolishness of God is wiser than men, and the weakness of God is stronger than men" (1 Corinthians

> *God doesn't make mistakes when He chooses seemingly unqualified candidates for His assignments.*

1:25 NKJV). This counterintuitive manner in which God works seems to be His favorite way of *ensuring* that we and everyone else know it's *not* us, our power, our strength, or our wisdom that gets results. On the contrary, Zechariah 4:6 (NKJV) says the following: "*Not* by might *nor* by power, but by My Spirit', says the Lord of *Hosts*" (emphasis own).

I emphasized a few words there because I find it so interesting that God is saying this specifically in His role as the "Lord of Hosts," which is the Commander-in-Chief of Heaven's Army: the most powerful and mighty thing imaginable! Watching the 101st in action gave me just the tiniest glimpse of what this would look like, and even that was pretty awesome. Yet He says it is *not* those things that accomplish great works in His Kingdom; it is Him and His *Spirit* alone. God says He will not share His glory with another (Isaiah 42:8), and this is one way of making it unequivocally clear Who was behind it.

For the longest time, this made me think of God as egotistical, prideful, and narcissistic. If He really is so high, mighty, exalted, and lifted up above us, why does he seem to need so badly to make this point? Would a grown man and father feel the need to constantly and emphatically state to his little children that everything good they had at home was only the result of *his* doing? Of course not, and Matthew 7:11 says that God is a good Father who knows how to give good gifts to His kids.

God is a good Father who knows how to give good gifts to His kids.

After a deeper revelation of God's goodness in my own life, I now believe He is so emphatic about us knowing that *He* is the One behind everything amazing and good that happens because He wants us to know a deeper and fuller measure of His almost unbelievable goodness, love, and heart for us, so that we *know* His nature and character based on our *experiences* in this life. The more clearly we are able to discern God's goodness toward us as the causal reason for our success, breakthrough, and blessing, the more securely we can rest in His love and good intentions for us, bringing us to a yet more full measure of His goodness.

Despite LTC Cooper's confidence and trust in me, I became even more tied up in knots and stressed out when I became the OIC of the DOMEX team at Andar. Because of a critical shortage of linguists in-theater, we had to outsource all of our translations to different bases in-theater. This sometimes took a long time because of the workload at the other locations, and I constantly felt like I was behind on our workload. I never felt like I was doing enough or had any confidence in my ability to lead the team effectively and add value to the unit I was supporting.

Because of this, every time material from a mission was brought back to us, I inwardly panicked and secretly wished they would never find anything to give us to work on. In turn, that sentiment made me feel terrible about the fact that I never wanted to do my job. The enemy had a field day in my mind, hurling all kinds of accusations against me about how lazy I was, what a terrible officer and leader I was, and what a disgrace I was to the military. I was praying fervently, waking up early to read the Word and journal, though I wasn't getting enough sleep as it was. Any semblance of peace, comfort, or rest I could gain from morning devotions immediately evaporated the second I walked into the tactical workspace as the grind ensued and the cortisol flooded my bloodstream.

Ironically, even though I was in a dangerous combat zone at a base that took incoming rockets and mortars multiple times every day, I was rarely if ever concerned for my physical safety. The crushing, self-imposed work performance anxiety I couldn't seem to escape left little room in my mind or heart for anything else. Somehow, though, OS2 Hawkins and I were able to get enough work done that apparently our chain of command saw fit to direct more resources our way, the first of which were desperately needed linguists.

No matter how impressive your analytical skills within the intel field may be, you were starting off dead in the water if you couldn't understand Pashto, Urdu, Dari, Farsi, or any other number of languages and local dialects that all of the raw intel appeared in. Because of the classified nature of the material, DOMEX linguists had to have a secret security clearance. This made them a mission-critical resource since there was a shortage of qualified linguists at the time, especially for intel units where the lack of at least a secret clearance was an immediate show-stopper.

Unfortunately, most of the linguists my team finally did receive were not nearly as proficient as their job descriptions indicated and required. They were *supposed* to be fluent in English and at least one of the other languages frequently spoken in that area, not just in listening and speaking for verbal conversations (which they generally were). Much more importantly for my unit's purposes, though, they needed to be fluent in reading and writing. This is hard for us to understand as native English speakers where there is almost universal standardization for the written word, but many of the dialects in that region are not written. As such, there are as many different ways to spell and use grammar for the same words and phrases as one's imagination allows for. I saw literally 20 to 30 different iterations of the name "Mohammed."

Moreover, none of them had any computer skills, so it was a painful and arduous process on my part to train them in the use of computers. You probably wouldn't believe this, but just a simple cut and paste operation is actually about ten steps if you really break it down, which I had to do over and over again. And even then, there were still numerous questions I had to ask and edits on my part after the fact that took a long time. With a high volume of material that needed to be translated at our location, I had a desperate need for at least two fully qualified linguists. All told, the learning curve to get a reasonably functional linguist up and running to the point where they were completely without my supervision was usually almost a month.

To make matters even worse, it was very difficult retaining linguists at Andar. I observed a painfully obvious entitlement mentality in most of the ones I was sent. Upon accepting the position with its generous compensation package, these linguists had been thoroughly briefed that their financial reward was commensurate with the risk. The reason they were being highly paid was because there was a distinct possibility they could be sent to hardship locations in dangerous areas where their lives could very well be in danger.

However, when many of them got to the cushy locations at the bigger bases with relatively good quality of life (like I had experienced at Bagram), they became accustomed to the quality of life at that location. Therefore, they did not have a good attitude when they got transferred to austere FOBs like Andar. I had several encounters with these linguists, who would show up for a week or maybe even just a couple days and do as little work as possible. They seemed to spend virtually all of their time and energy finding some loophole or illegitimate reason as to why they could not stay and were soon transferred elsewhere.

Spending so much time training, and then promptly losing, so many interpreters became extremely frustrating and inefficient. It gives new meaning to the term "lost in translation." It felt like we were never going to make any progress. Meanwhile, the enemy certainly wasn't taking a break. The workload continued to increase, and I felt like we were getting further and further behind. The anxiety kept building, and I was coming to my wit's end. I already felt unqualified and ill-equipped before I was given my own team, but I felt even more so now.

But again, God doesn't call the qualified. He qualifies and equips those whom He has called for whatever assignment He's given them. I was about to find out just how true that is.

PERSONAL REFLECTION AND PRACTICAL APPLICATION

Do you feel like you're isolated, overwhelmed, or otherwise out of your element? Are you having trouble accepting an "assignment" or calling in life for which you're unqualified or ill-equipped? Be encouraged by Paul's words in 1 Corinthians 1:26–27: "For you see your calling, brethren, that not many wise according to the flesh, not many mighty, not many noble, are called. God is using the foolish things of the world put to shame the wise, and God's chosen the weak things of the world put to shame the things which are mighty..." The sooner you can embrace getting to the end of yourself, the sooner you release God's mighty power to work *for* you.

CHAPTER 6

HUMILITY FOR STRENGTH AND STRENGTH FOR HUMILITY

In the midst of my frustration, inadequacy, and anxiety, God began to bless me. This blessing came in the form of several people: highly valuable and sorely needed members of the team at Andar. I was overjoyed when we got our first one, Ashkan Jan. Ashkan had a warm smile and a gentle demeanor. He had grown up in Afghanistan and emigrated to the United States during the Russian invasion several decades before. Ashkan became a naturalized American citizen and had been working full-time in America for many years and was now raising a family in the expensive Washington D.C. metro area.

Because he had a security clearance, he was eligible for and ended up taking what looked to him to be a great opportunity as a well-compensated US combat linguist. In this role, he could not only support his family financially but could also help Coalition Forces fight against the Taliban and other terrorist/ extremist insurgent groups who he felt were the archenemy to what he expressed as his peace-loving religion of Islam as well as his native land and people.

The vehement response that he and a few other native Afghan linguists had towards the Taliban left a distinctive impression on me. Their anger burned deeper, longer, and hotter against our enemy than that of even the most battle-hardened infantry soldiers in our unit. After some long and heartfelt spiritual conversations with another linguist named Azari who joined our team, I found out why.

Like Ashkan, Azari was born and raised in Afghanistan. He came from a very wealthy and politically well-connected family, enjoying a life of privilege and affluence but also one of deep familial love and connection. He had just graduated from law school, but on the exact day he was scheduled to take the Afghan equivalent of the bar exam to become a practicing lawyer, he had to flee the country for his life during that same period of war and political upheaval. He came to America where he started at the bottom rung of the socioeconomic ladder without any family or political connections, his impressive pedigree, or even the ability to speak the language. He eventually assimilated into American culture, learned the language, and became a car salesman and naturalized citizen.

He too saw an opportunity to provide for his family as a combat linguist. Perhaps even more than most, Azari was a very devout Muslim who loved and cherished the Qur'an, Islam, and most of all, his personal relationship with Allah. My only perception of Muslims at that time was that, at best, the majority of Muslims were just caught in the spirit of religion by outwardly observing deeply ingrained cultural and historic practices that didn't truly have a profound impact on their hearts and lives. The only ones I saw who *did* seem to truly give their lives for the sake of Allah and Islam were the ones doing so literally as martyrs, by crashing into and/or blowing up skyscrapers, US military checkpoints, and crowded markets surrounded by innocent women and children and constructing lethal roadside bombs that were killing thousands of my fellow brothers in arms.

But Azari challenged my perception of Muslims as being either misled victims under the oppressive yoke of religious bondage or intolerant and violent extremists whose only expression of faith was death and destruction. He is one of the kindest, gentlest, most sincere, and spiritual men I have ever met. In addition to outwardly observing the many and frequent daily rituals of Islam, Azari had a deep reverence for Allah, demonstrated through his frequent personal time in prayer and reading the Qur'an.

As I spent more time with him and got to know him more, we began to have deep and meaningful personal conversations during which we shared our respective faiths. Azari's s faith was clearly much more than an empty, outwardly legalistic routine. It was something vital, alive, and meaningful to him. One day, he shared with me something that he heard in his personal prayer time with Allah earlier that morning: "Azari, when you have Me, you have *everything*." Wow… that sounded nothing like the "Allah" shouted by the jihadists immediately before they took so many innocent lives along with their own.

That is why Azari would get almost apoplectic when he saw and heard the atrocities the Taliban and other insurgents were perpetrating in the name of Allah. "This is **not** the work of Allah! *These* [insurgents] are the infidels!!" he would yell. These kinds of outrages seemed to kindle within him a holy fire to "remove these guys from the battlefield," as we said. That fire in his belly to be part of the fight drove Azari almost in ways I imagine the Apostle Paul was driven in his mission for God. He demonstrated this from the time he got to our unit.

When Azari was assigned to my unit, I quickly discovered that he was in his early 60s and was missing part of his gallbladder. This caused him to need to use the bathroom multiple times in the middle of the night, *every* single night. At this time, it was the middle of winter at 7000 feet of elevation with three feet of snow, and we still had no flushing toilets and were living in tents. This meant he had to get out of bed, put on multiple layers of clothes, including his body armor, and go number two in a bag in the pitch dark. Given the litany of asinine reasons other interpreters had recently found to weasel their way out of staying at Andar, I had about as much hope of Azari staying on with us for more than about 12 hours as I did of being personally spot promoted to Commanding General of the Afghanistan theater.

I was surprised and impressed to find him still with us after the first night. I attributed it to a fluke and assumed that at any minute I'd be informed of his inevitable transfer. If anyone had a legitimate reason for leaving, it was definitely Azari. After three days or so, I was really wondering what was going on. What was this guy still doing here?! In addition to the fact that he had a strong initial rapport with Ashkan (who was also miraculously with us after several months), I believe it was the fire in his belly and his sense of personal mission for Islam that caused him to stay with us and fight the "true infidels." Either way, it was God's Grace for me because I was getting to the end of my rope with the linguist situation and the workload.

That being said, God was clearly giving us grace and favor, as resources and members were slowly added to the team. In addition to Ashkan and Azari, I was sent another enlisted sailor who was extremely valuable and helpful to the team. OS1 Kirk Pilfer arrived a few months after we got there and contributed greatly. In addition to training the linguists on how to use the computer, I was also training OS2 Hawkins and OS1 Pilfer on proper procedures and the most effective way to write the intel reports, which were the primary output, or deliverables, of our activity.

For deployments longer than nine months, military personnel stationed in a designated combat zone are allowed rest and recuperation (R&R) leave at some point on their tour.

Mine was scheduled for January, when I would be meeting my family in southeast Asia. Because of travel difficulties, I was gone for an entire month. Before I left, the highest priority was ensuring the success of our team. It was crucially important they felt trained and equipped to operate seamlessly without any other direct supervision.

One of the proudest moments I had in my entire Navy career was when I got back from R&R. I returned to an email inbox flooded with the highest accolades for Hawkins and Pilfer. They had truly distinguished themselves and our team. On more than one occasion, their reports were specifically selected for division-level intelligence briefings at Bagram with some of the most senior General Officers in the country attending. After the second or third time this happened, I specifically remember an email from my immediate superior in Bagram that said, "You guys are on a roll..." Indeed, they were.

As a leader, one of the most satisfying and rewarding experiences is preparing your men and women for success and being able to celebrate it when it occurs. To this day, it makes me still want to shed a tear for how proud I was of my guys and our entire team. Despite all my stress, toil, and anxiety, it appeared that what had started as a humble two-man team without even our own interpreter was increasing in recognition and resources.

However, notoriety and acclaim is not what I was looking for. I was still just trying to keep my head above water with the anxiety that still affected me every day. While I was on leave, I talked to my dad about it and described the difficulties I had experienced in the last four months or so and my apprehension about the next seven I would endure after I returned.

My dad had experienced severe anxiety and even panic attacks that were related to work performance anxiety after a similar situation where he opened a new office in a new location for his job. It's hard to explain to someone who hasn't experienced intense and protracted anxiety before, but the fact that he and I were able to so clearly relate to and understand the thoughts, feelings, and struggles it entails was extremely cathartic and therapeutic for me.

From a spiritual perspective, I was conflicted about how to approach this. I knew clearly that anxiety and stress are not from God, and I felt like I was doing everything I could on a practical and spiritual level to fight it other than seeing a psychiatrist and getting medication. I had considered medication but felt like it was neither God's best for me nor necessary with the power of the Holy Spirit within me. I felt like I just needed to try harder in exercising my faith to overcome this. For some reason, though, I couldn't seem to translate my faith and prayers to a steady emotional and mental state at work.

My dad said that he thought the exact same way when he was younger, but when he finally got so desperate that he broke down enough to see a counselor and got medication, he wished he had never wasted that time in the first place under the misguided notion that it made him less of a man or less of a Christian to do so. He strongly encouraged me not to make the same mistake and suffer needlessly. Despite some initial reluctance, I followed his advice and made an appointment with the psychiatrist at one of the bases on my way back from leave en route to Andar.

I was prescribed an antidepressant medication called Zoloft, which can also help with anxiety. It can sometimes actually exacerbate symptoms before it alleviates them, and I may have experienced some of that the first few days I got back. Objectively, we didn't have all that much going on, but my anxiety was overwhelming. One night, it got so bad that I was literally at the point I felt like I needed to have my chain of command remove and replace me with someone else who was more fit for the job.

Even now as I write this, it seems so silly when I objectively think about it. But when you're in the middle of that hamster wheel, logic and reason offer no solace. I remember making one final desperate plea to God as I prayed for some kind of help that would preclude such an embarrassing and unprofessional request. 1 Peter 5:6–7 (NIV) says, "Humble yourselves, therefore, under God's mighty hand, that he may lift you up in due time. Cast all your anxiety on him because he cares for you."

Due time, indeed! With God as my witness, the very *next day,* God sent what seemed like an angel to me to answer my desperate prayer, and his name was Ron Tillman. Ron was a civilian Media Exploitation Technician (MEDEX tech) who'd been assigned to my team while I was on leave. He also happened to be an Army Reserve Warrant Officer and was intimately familiar with the Army.

Ron was an absolute computer genius and an amazing asset to work with, but even more than that, he was a fellow believer who I could talk to about my struggles as well as my faith. Because of his

> *"Cast all your anxiety on him because he cares for you."*

depth of experience as an enlisted person and his experience in leadership as a Warrant Officer, he was also a perfect go-between for me and my enlisted guys if they felt like they needed to speak frankly about issues they were having but were not comfortable telling me directly. The fact that he was on our team as a civilian made that dynamic even more relaxed and informal.

Ron was also able to unburden himself to me about some issues he had in the past that still were causing him to fall under guilt and condemnation at times as well as some current issues that were bothering him. It was a perfect example of the incredible blessing of fellowship with another believer and the way that it can unburden both people's hearts. Instantly, the dynamic changed, and I had a much more positive outlook on things. It took awhile to take effect, but the medication did start to help, although it did not completely solve my anxiety. All of this could not have come at a better time, because we were about to get absolutely slammed for the next several months.

Some military personnel on our base observed suspicious activity from the local nationals who worked on the FOB. In what I personally believe was a misguided attempt at local economic development and winning the hearts and minds of the local populace, the US government contracted with companies who would hire local nationals to perform various tasks on the military bases such as waste and trash removal and other janitorial type services, but these positions also included contract security personnel who would man the potentially deadly 50-caliber machine guns in the lookout towers.

This was to augment the shifts for soldiers on guard duty and lessen the demands of having to stand watch 24/7. The issue with this was that there were known Taliban insurgents who had repeatedly attempted to, and several times been successful in, infiltrating Coalition Forces bases and initiating complex attacks that were sometimes devastatingly lethal. (I sometimes imagine what World War II veterans must've thought of such practices if they were told that Nazis would be manning the machine guns of Allied Forces bases.)

After enough suspicious incidents, the battalion ordered a FOB-wide sweep of all documents and media belonging to local nationals, not just on our base but on all the other outlying bases the other battalion occupied. It was an overwhelming amount of material to process, but we were able to get through it, and it yielded some incredibly valuable intelligence. After combing through all the evidence and data from the DOMEX process, we identified 11 individuals we considered to be highly suspicious. These 11 "persons of interest" were detained and sent to another base for "tactical questioning" (the politically correct term for "interrogation") by experienced counter-intelligence agents and law enforcement professionals.

During this questioning, several of those detainees eventually admitted to being Taliban insurgents and revealed a plan to detonate a bomb in the middle of the base I worked on and then turn the guard tower machine guns inward to kill as many of us as possible. Within less than a week of the day that was planned to occur, we had exposed and neutralized that threat. We had just potentially saved hundreds of lives on our base, including our own. After months of grinding it out and not really seeing many direct and critically important results from our efforts, that provided an amazing sense of job satisfaction and achievement for our entire team as well as a sobering reminder of the dangerous reality we all faced on a daily basis.

This also was a huge win for LTC Cooper and the overall DOMEX program in clearly demonstrating the value our teams could bring the Army units to which we were assigned. It was also a high return on investment for the decision LTC Cooper had made in selecting me as a very unlikely team lead as well as for significantly increasing the size and resources of our team. What had started out with just OS2 Hawkins and myself was now officially resourced as a fully outfitted six-person team: one officer, two enlisted personnel, two linguists, and one civilian MEDEX tech with a full MEDEX suite of equipment.

I also received a very favorable performance evaluation for my assignment. I ended up being ranked number two out of ten within my peer group, received an "early promote" recommendation board (the highest possible recommendation), and a near-perfect numerical report average. Everybody besides LTC Cooper—most of all, me—was pleasantly shocked by how well I did in an extremely difficult and dangerous assignment.

This helped me gain a sense of personal and professional redemption after experiencing spectacular failure for the first half of my Navy career. By this point, I knew it was not about me and my performance; it was about a faithful and good Father who had consistently protected and provided for me my entire life. I was not going to make the mistake that Moses warned the Israelites about in Deuteronomy 8 by becoming prideful and arrogant in assuming that it was my power or the strength of my hands that accomplished this. I had been humbled enough to recognize it was only "by His Spirit" that any of this was possible.

Shortly before I left FOB Andar, I was given an opportunity to demonstrate this humility in a confrontation I had with the Battalion Intel Officer. This had been brewing for a while and finally came to ahead about a month before I finished my deployment. To my team and many other outside personnel attached to this Army unit, there was a marked contrast in the professionalism and productivity between the 101st and this new unit, particularly in the intel shop where my team and I worked. I'll just say it was not a conducive atmosphere to getting work done. One of the things that frustrated me the most, though, was the profane language. I understood and accepted the fact that I was with infantry soldiers in an Army infantry unit. As such, their use of profanity was and will always be frequent, enthusiastic, and simply a part of their culture (and to be fair, we sailors don't exactly have a sterling reputation for sterile language either).

What I took issue with and mentioned several times (as the ranking military officer in the room, no less) was that it was offensive and unprofessional for them to use the Lord's name in vain so often and that I was politely but firmly asking them to cease and desist in doing so. Later, a brief was given on Army regulations that specifically stated a unit member had the right to lodge a formal complaint for precisely such language.

I did not do so but pointed out the fact that their own Army regulations prohibited this type of profanity.

While he himself was an extremely sharp, motivated, and professional Officer, the S2 of this battalion (who held the same rank as me but was significantly junior to me as far as time in rank was concerned) spent all of his time down the hall in another room and rarely had direct observation of the general lack of professionalism and productivity that his subordinates consistently demonstrated. That being said, I find it hard to imagine that he didn't have an inkling of what was going on with his guys. Even if he didn't, I considered that in itself as a leadership deficit on his part. For all these reasons, I was absolutely shocked and outraged when he fired off an email to me one day that included a laundry list of accusations against me for my perceived lack of professionalism and productivity and the assertion that there had been talk of a formal complaint lodged against me from his team.

If anyone were to lodge a formal complaint, I felt it certainly would have been me. I had more than enough evidence and witnesses to stage a potentially decimating full-scale counterattack to his arguments and claims. But as I was leading a Bible study at the time, talking to my brothers in Christ, and journaling every day with the Holy Spirit, I knew deep down that this was not the kind of response Jesus would give. Even though it was offensive and unwelcome at the time he initially said it, a wise Navy Chief (senior enlisted leader) of another unit on the base reminded me of what Jesus said at the Sermon on the Mount:

> Blessed are the peacemakers, for they shall be called sons of God. Blessed are those who have been persecuted for the sake of righteousness, for theirs is the kingdom of heaven. Blessed are you when people insult you and persecute you, and falsely say all kinds of evil against you because of Me.

Rejoice and be glad, for your reward in heaven is great; for in the same way they persecuted the prophets who were before you. (Matthew 5:9–12, NASB)

As much as I hated it, I knew the Chief was right (whether or not he would have responded the same way if he were in my shoes). Luckily, I had waited before I fired back a scathing response to the S2's email. As I searched my soul and gave the Holy Spirit access to my heart and mind during this time, I was aware that I was in the enviable position of being about to go back home. I knew that all this would do is create strife and dissension right before the next Navy team relieved us. That was not the handoff I wanted to give them.

Earlier, I quoted 1 Peter 5:6–7 about humbling myself before God in desperation, casting my cares on Him, and being exalted in due time. However, right before that (in verse 5), the Amplified Bible says this:

Likewise, you who are younger and of lesser rank, be subject to the elders (the ministers and spiritual guides of the church)—[giving them due respect and yielding to their counsel]. Clothe (apron) yourselves, all of you, with humility [as the garb of a servant, so that its covering cannot possibly be stripped from you, with freedom from pride and arrogance] toward one another. For God sets Himself against the proud (the insolent, the overbearing, the disdainful, the presumptuous, the boastful)—[and He opposes, frustrates, and defeats them], but gives grace (favor, blessing) to the humble.

Despite it going against the grain of every fiber of my flesh, I finally yielded to the Spirit and responded with a humble and unconditional apology to the S2. This felt like eating a heaping portion of humble pie, and I felt like a dog with its tail between his legs for no good reason. It took divine strength of character beyond what I possessed to do this. Immediately after I apologized, though, I had a peace and calm wash over me that I'll never forget. I had the thought in my head: "How much **better** it is to do things **God's** way." Things were immediately smoothed over with the S2, and I was able to give a smooth and peaceful handoff to my replacement when he got there.

Finally, my time of testing in the desert was over. Like Jesus, God baptized me with the Holy Spirit before a season of testing in the desert. I endured more than I thought I could possibly handle and had very nearly been totally

> *"How much **better** it is to do things **God's** way."*

broken. I had experienced both aspects of 1 Peter 5:5–7. When I was completely overwhelmed and about to quit, I needed to humble myself before God, casting all my anxiety and cares on Him, and trust Him to exalt me in due time. With the addition of wonderful people, He exalted us with favor, resources, increase, and redemption.

This season finally ended under His meekness with a response that totally flew in the face of human logic but indeed proved that "the weakness of God is stronger than men." I needed God's supernatural power and strength to reign over my flesh so I could humble myself *completely* to another person for the sake of making peace. So you can say it this way: **I needed humility for strength and strength for humility**. By His grace, God gave me both.

And also like Jesus, it was now time to leave the desert, be refreshed, and go back home.

Personal Reflection and Practical Application

If you're going through a really stressful time and dealing with a lot of anxiety, pour out your heart honestly before the Lord and ask Him for help and strength: "Humble yourselves, therefore, under God's mighty hand, that he may lift you up in due time. Cast all your anxiety on him because he cares for you" (1 Peter 5:6–7). Sometimes, the most significant help God gives in "due time" is through the right person at just the right moment, like I experienced with Ron. That prayer of heartfelt desperation can work a miraculous blessing at just the right time! Is there a situation with someone for which you need the Holy Spirit's power to humble yourself completely for the greater good (even—and especially—if you're *not* in the wrong)? 1 Peter 5:5 says: "All of you, clothe yourselves with humility toward one another, because 'God opposes the proud but shows favor to the humble.'" God's grace and Holy Spirit will give you humility for strength and strength for humility.

CHAPTER 7

BE NOT CONFORMED
TO THIS WORLD

I got home from Afghanistan in early August 2011. It would turn out to be a much-needed opportunity to rest and catch my breath. My time in Afghanistan was technically considered a form of "temporary" orders away from my parent command, which was the John C. Stennis aircraft carrier. The Stennis had just left for a nine-month deployment right before I got back. The military has a mandatory "dwell time" policy after deployments, during which you cannot be forced to immediately deploy again within a certain timeframe. I could have waived my dwell time and deployed with the Stennis, but I decided not to.

Though I was exhausted from my deployment to Afghanistan, part of me still felt it was my duty and obligation to suck it up and go back out to sea with my ship. However, I was finally learning to invest in rest. So I decided to accept the gift I had been given by relaxing and enjoying myself, as well as prepare for the next season of life. So I enjoyed a very restful five months of doing a "phone muster," which simply entailed checking in to work by phone every weekday morning to report that I was still alive and well. Talk about a change in battle rhythm!

That time was good for me. No longer under the extreme stress and anxiety from work, I gradually weaned myself off the anxiety medication I had been taking for the last six months. Thankfully, I had not experienced any acute combat trauma or post-traumatic stress that affects so many returning combat veterans. I did notice that, for some reason, I was having real difficulty adjusting to a regular sleep cycle once I got back, but taking a prescribed sleep medication for several months assisted with the transition. Other than that, I took care of myself naturally by eating healthy and going to the gym for several hours each day. I also cared for myself spiritually as I continued going to my Celebrate Recovery 12-step group and got back into church.

Another thing I did shortly after I got back was schedule an appointment with a career counselor my mom recommended. While deployed, I began to seriously consider my future career path and what I should do with it when I returned. Though I had a great performance evaluation from Afghanistan, I still had not done a lateral transfer to another community within the Navy, so I was classified as a General Aviation Officer. This is a type of holding category for former pilots like myself who are no longer in a flight status. Staying in General Aviation was not a viable career path if I wanted to get promoted and stay in the Navy long-term. I began to weigh the possibilities, both in and out of the Navy.

With this in mind, I attended my career counseling appointment with the man my mom had referred me to. He was a fellow veteran (of the Vietnam war) and was able to relate to my deployment experience. He was also a Christian and had built a successful business practice within the realm of his strength, which was helping other people to discover and live out their own strengths and career paths. His framework led to meaningful insights that gave me a further sense of passion, direction, and focus for identifying my life's purpose and how God uniquely designed me for fulfillment.

This new perspective influenced several major decisions over the next few years. For starters, I realized that my Navy career path probably couldn't give me the fulfillment I truly desired, so I began to consider and then plan for what I would do when I separated from military service. After five restful months of dwell time in Bremerton, Washington, my next set of orders was to the Pentagon in Washington, D.C. I was assigned to the Staff of the Chief of Naval Operations, which programs the Navy's budget. I requested this set of orders because I wanted to use my Master in Business to set myself up for a good post-military career. Working as a defense budget analyst at the Pentagon could provide connections to lucrative opportunities in the private sector as a defense contractor or financial manager.

I got to the Pentagon in early 2012 for what would be my last set of military orders. I was assigned as a Navy Manpower Requirements Officer, managing a $4.5 billion budget for 60,000 personnel positions. The learning curve was very steep, and anxiety began to creep in. Having learned from my experience in Afghanistan, I didn't hesitate in seeking help from a counselor and getting prescribed medication. It helped to a degree, but the new position was still a struggle. More than the anxiety, though, I faced a profound sense of professional unfulfillment. There was no passion or personal connection to my work. I felt like an insignificant cog in a massive bureaucratic wheel, stuck in a cubicle every day crunching numbers on spreadsheets and cranking out PowerPoint presentations.

I knew at some level that the work we were doing was important. We were making decisions for prioritizing the funding and equipping of frontline warfighters, but it felt so disconnected from any direct impact. There were many urgent deadlines for supposedly critical tasks that didn't seem to ultimately accomplish anything of discernible or meaningful value. This vexing dichotomy between activity and perceived impact made it hard to maintain motivation or the sense that anything I did actually mattered, like a tiny drop in a vast bucket of data and decisions. I felt bad for having this attitude, which only made things worse.

Outside of work, though, I was finding more personal meaning, passion, and connection than I ever had before. I was attending a small charismatic church in Virginia, much like the one where I received the baptism of the Holy Spirit in Oregon before going to Afghanistan. They fully embraced the supernatural gifts of the Holy Spirit, and everyone in the congregation was on fire for the things of God. I felt at home the second I walked in and quickly established some of the deepest and most profound personal connections of my life.

It was in a small group from this church that I experienced this life-giving connection most powerfully. The church was relatively new and small when I joined, so they hadn't yet established any formal programs or groups. Because of this, in the first service I attended, the pastor encouraged us to informally get into small groups for greater connection within the church. A group of us followed his advice by sharing our contact information, and I offered to host the group at my house. Like me, most of the others in this group had been born again at an early age and gone to church for a long time. But almost all of us seemed to be in a similar season of newfound hunger and passion for God, primarily from a recent revelation and personal experience of God's supernatural power.

Our shared spiritual hunger and expectation created a contagiously powerful atmosphere, resulting in deep connections that were established very quickly. We decided early on that this wasn't going to be "just another Bible study" or religious program. We wanted to let the Holy Spirit lead this group in whatever way *He* wanted to, so we made room for Him to do so. Practically, this manifested as more of an emphasis on prayer and personal sharing. We would include musical worship and share whatever passages of scripture came to mind if and when we felt prompted by the Spirit. Prayer requests and answers to prayer were something we emphasized sharing regularly.

Because of this, there was an authenticity and vulnerability that created a strong sense of community and connection. We all wanted to be there and looked forward to going. I never thought I could be so genuinely *excited* about God and "church stuff." As a result, we naturally shared this with other friends and acquaintances who started coming to the group. At first, we were mainly young single professionals in our 20s and 30s. But as time went on, people of all ages and backgrounds started coming. Many of us who would not otherwise normally socialize with each other became very close friends because of our spiritual connection. It was a beautiful thing to see God's Spirit bring people together.

Within about six months, what started out with four of us in our first small group meeting had grown to about 45 people showing up on any given week. We had about 70 people on an email list and established four different "ministries" within the small group: an inner healing and deliverance prayer team, a homeless outreach in downtown D.C., a worship team, and a hospitality team that coordinated food for "family dinner." We had rapidly grown from a small group to a large group and then to what was essentially a home church.

> *I never thought I could be so genuinely excited about God and "church stuff."*

The amazing thing was that it all happened completely organically. We had no intentions of making this a big group or starting a home church. We just shared a common desire to experience more of God in our personal lives and in community, and the Holy Spirit naturally/supernaturally facilitated the increase. At some point fairly early on as we were growing rapidly, it became apparent that some kind of leadership would be good and necessary. I felt like the Holy Spirit had been speaking to me about this, so when someone mentioned it out loud one week, I stepped into the role.

This was a formative growth period for me spiritually and as a leader more than any other time in my entire life, including my military experience. This magnitude of growth was true for many others in the group as well. As one of my close friends would later say, these times were "the wonder years" of personal and spiritual growth in our relationships with God and each other. He also referred to this group as being like "the fellowship of the ring" that Tolkien wrote about, in that we were bound together on an adventure, even a quest, of great and noble import.

The contrast in my heart-level engagement between work and the small group was instructive. Despite the professional and financial opportunities, I finally realized that I didn't want to go into a defense contracting role after I got out of the military. In early 2013, I put in my official separation request to get out of the Navy as soon as my service commitment was complete at the end of that year. Meanwhile, I was more alive and fulfilled in a relational ministry context through the small group than I ever had been before. I also continued the journey of investigation with God about my deepest passions, greatest gifts, and a way to incorporate those into a fulfilling line of work.

I read a book called *Work by Referral* by Brian Buffini and Joe Niego. Brian had been a successful realtor for years and transitioned into coaching others in the real estate industry. His book talked about how much more relational, enjoyable, and profitable it is to build one's business working exclusively by personal referrals from friends and family members. This approach really appealed to me. I really liked the idea of the entrepreneurial freedom and flexibility to integrate my work with my personal life and relationships.

I went back over my report from the career counselor I worked with and was surprised to see that working as a real estate agent was one of his top recommendations for me. He believed a career along those lines would be good for me because of a combination of factors: regularly getting outside of the office, relational connection,

We can be "full-time ministers" as employees, business owners/entrepreneurs, government officials, or any other occupation.

goal orientation, freedom, and high income potential. My experience at the Pentagon definitely confirmed an office job spending most of my time behind a desk wasn't an option. And the small group confirmed my passion and the life-giving benefits I experienced from regularly and deeply connecting with people.

I seriously considered becoming a pastor or something in a "full-time ministry" role, but I doubted that would scratch the itch of my very practical and achievement-oriented personality. I realized I wanted something that afforded the option to combine ministry and business. I've since come to know that "ministry" simply means "service" and is not confined to being a pastor, preacher, missionary, or any other traditional "ministry" role. We can be "full-time ministers" as employees, business owners/ entrepreneurs, government officials, or any other occupation. In fact, we need full-time ministers in these other occupations.

With this new perspective in mind, I felt led to get my license and become a realtor. This wasn't something I had ever thought about or previously desired, but I wanted to try something totally different from what I had been doing in the Navy or a traditional corporate job. I couldn't wait to move on to an exciting new season of life and professional fulfillment.

Throughout my two years at the Pentagon, I would often get frustrated and ask God why I was in that job. Toward the end of that assignment, I became more aware of and grateful for all the benefits that job and my years of military service offered. I was making a high income with a great benefits package, a lot of time off with 30 days of military "leave" (paid vacation) per year, valuable professional experience, a great resume, and veterans benefits that would give me financial freedom and opportunities once I left the military.

Perhaps an even greater benefit was that of **perspective**. My greatest struggle was in keeping a good attitude and perspective until I left that job. I felt like I was under the bondage of "professional Egypt" and couldn't *wait* to get to the Promised Land. On a spiritual level, the Lord blessed me with perspective when He spoke this to my heart:

> *Ryan, you think your frustration and dissatisfaction right now is working against you. In truth, it is working powerfully **for** you. It needs to be so deeply ingrained in you that what you have right now is not personally fulfilling. Therefore, when you're wandering through the desert on the way to your Promised Land, you'll never once look back and long for the days of Egypt like the Israelites did. You will be grateful for the manna you live on day by day in the wilderness because you're no longer in Egypt. **Remember** this time right now; **do not forget it** as you are on your way to the Promised Land.*

That was so true. Because that frustration and dissatisfaction was so deeply drilled into me for what felt like forever, I never *once* regretted my decision to leave the Navy or the possibility of a high-paying corporate job during the lean times that followed. After I left the Navy, sometimes I'd go back to visit my old coworkers at the Pentagon and catch up. They'd be in the middle of a budget cycle, and I'd be so grateful I wasn't there doing that anymore, even without the nice paycheck and benefits that went with it.

On a more practical level, I was blessed by the perspective at a relatively young age that a "good job" provided much more than high income, position and title, job security, and generous paid time off. I saw many people who were miserable with their work, going through the motions of "punching their time card" until they could receive their second or even third retirement and "finally enjoy life." Meanwhile, their health was deteriorating as they were becoming more unfulfilled and professionally disengaged each day at work. In my opinion, they had become imprisoned by the insidious comfortable mediocrity of security and stability from a well-paying job, only to realize too late that it didn't give them what they really wanted out of life.

The world is constantly trying to fit us into its mold. Our modern American culture teaches and conditions us to get good grades, go to a good school, and get a "good job" (which many people don't enjoy). We're taught that after plugging away at a job for 30 to 40 years, we can finally enjoy our lives in retirement, at which point we'll be old and wish we could enjoy our youth again. Especially for men (but now also increasingly for women), there's a pervasive tendency to sacrifice family, health, relationships, and personal dreams on the altar of career advancement and "success." On their deathbed, most people who fall victim to this deception won't wish they had spent more time at the office and made more money.

The world is constantly trying to fit us into its mold.

They'll regret not spending more time with their family and friends, truly enjoying life.

This is what Jesus referred to in Mark 4:19 by the "deceitfulness of riches:" money, achievement, and "success" deceive us by promising something they can never deliver. Meanwhile, our pursuit for these lesser things distract and keep us from what is truly life-giving and important. I decided that this version of the American Dream was not for me. I refused to let the world fit me into its mold. Romans 12:2 (KJV) says, "... **be not conformed to this world...**" I love the way this verse is worded in The Passion Translation: **"Stop imitating the ideals and opinions of the culture around you, but be inwardly transformed by the Holy Spirit through a total reformation of how you think. This will empower you to discern God's will as you live a beautiful life, satisfying and perfect in his eyes."**

We don't have to settle for our culture's definition of success; there is a better way! We can be fully alive, highly productive, well-compensated, and serve others by doing what we truly love and are naturally good at (something I'll talk about in more depth in

Money, achievement, and "success" deceive us by promising something they can never deliver.

Chapter 23). We don't have to sacrifice relationships, health, or personal fulfillment to earn a good living, nor do we have to take a vow of poverty and asceticism to do the Lord's work. We can be simultaneously profitable *and* purposeful in our work. We'll talk more about this in future chapters, but God *wants* to bless and prosper us in accomplishing His good purposes for our lives!

There may be sacrifices and lifestyle adjustments on the way to accomplishing those dreams and purposes. Most things that are truly valuable require making a sacrifice. But the sacrifice is worth it! And even that sacrificial process doesn't have to be a difficult exercise based on self-effort. I knew I'd need to make a significant downward lifestyle adjustment after I got out of the military, but it wasn't a hard decision in the *least*— at the time, or even later on. God gave me the grace to make that decision, even if it was partly through dissatisfaction and frustration. God is not the Author of dissatisfaction, frustration, anxiety, or anything else harmful, but He absolutely can and will use it for our benefit.

God intends for work to be a blessing!

God intends for work to be a *blessing*! Our personal vocation can and *should* be something in which we are fully alive; giving us opportunities to make a meaningful impact to individuals and the world at large. What God's Kingdom and way of life offers is so much more and so much better than what the world offers. Don't settle for less than God's *best* for your life!

PERSONAL REFLECTION AND PRACTICAL APPLICATION

Are you chasing the world's definition of success, falling victim to the deceitfulness of riches by sacrificing what's truly important for things that will never satisfy you? Are you spinning your wheels, trapped in the prison of comfortable mediocrity? Don't allow the world to conform you to its mold. Meditate on Romans 12:2 (TPT): "Stop imitating the ideals and opinions of the culture around you, but be inwardly transformed by the Holy Spirit through a total reformation of how you think. This will empower you to discern God's will as you live a beautiful life, satisfying and perfect in his eyes." God has so much more for you than what this world can offer; don't settle for less than His best for you!

CHAPTER 8

THE UNFORCED RHYTHMS OF GRACE

My separation orders had my official last day of military service as February 1, 2014. I was scheduled to go on "terminal leave" right before Thanksgiving in 2013. Terminal leave starts when you get your orders stamped for your last day of duty, after which the rest of your time in the military is on "leave" (paid vacation). In preparation for leaving the Navy, there were a lot of things that had to line up in the next few months. I needed to find a roommate to replace me on my current lease.

I needed to schedule my final household goods move with the Navy, which I was hesitant to do without having found someone to replace me on my current lease for the apartment I was living in. I could not wait much longer without risking the chance they wouldn't have an availability for the day I needed. I also did not know where I would be living afterward, but I knew that I was going to need to significantly downsize my quality of living after my nice Navy paycheck went away. Finally, I really wanted to travel overseas during my terminal leave, but there were a lot of things that needed to get done to make that happen.

I was getting stressed and anxious, but as I was praying, I felt like the Lord brought an image to my mind: I was taking a step forward with nothing in front of me, but right before my foot hit the ground, a perfectly laid brick path would appear. This was a perfect visual representation of what happened, just taking one small step of faith after the next. I scheduled my household goods move for a convenient day, trusting the Lord would send a suitable replacement to take my spot in the apartment. Sure enough, we found a great person who got along with my existing roommates to replace me on my lease.

At about the same time, a friend named John called and asked me if I might pray about possibly living in a spare bedroom in his house, which would only cost me $500 per month (a rare find in the sky-high D.C. area housing market!). This would be a mutual blessing, as it gave me cheap rent while also helping him supplement income for his family. As a Christmas present, my parents were able to offer me a week of their timeshare to stay in Europe, which opened up miraculously at the last second after trying multiple times with no luck. Most times, these places are booked anywhere from six to 18 months in advance. God was proving to me that what He had shown me in that mental image during prayer could be trusted as I just took small steps of faith for His practical answers and provision to my logistical needs.

As part of the Transition Assistance Program in preparation for military separation, I had been told to have a Veteran Service Organization review my medical records. With their expertise, they submitted an application on my behalf to Veterans Affairs (VA) for potential compensation I may be eligible for as a result of different service-connected medical conditions. A critical part of this process is completing what's called a Compensation and Pension Physical Examination, or "C&P exam." I was told that it was really important to get this done *before* separating from active-duty service. Otherwise, it could take years to get an adjudication on the VA's decision.

I was on terminal leave trying to schedule my physical exam before going home for Christmas with my family and then being out of the country for the rest of my terminal leave. I basically had to get my exam done within the next week, or it would not get done until I was out of the military. I was calling everybody I knew and doing everything I could to get this exam scheduled, but to no avail. I was getting incredibly frustrated and anxious about this. After half a day of fruitlessly pounding my head against a wall with no results, I finally threw up my hands in frustration and prayed to the Lord, saying that I was officially giving up and leaving this in His hands.

I kid you not, at that *exact instant*, my phone rang. It was literally like that prayer and decision to let go and leave it to God pushed an invisible button that caused my phone to ring. On the other end of the line, it was the *exact person* I needed to get in touch with to schedule my exam. I was able to get that done within the week before leaving the area, and as a result, I had a miraculously fast VA decision.

This provided monthly payments immediately upon leaving the Navy that have been an incredible blessing God has used to financially support me in my post-Navy life. It has also given me the freedom to make decisions from a place of being led by my heart's desires as opposed to financial necessity. This was an immediate and spectacular demonstration to me that "rest finds grace (unmerited favor)," as Pastor Joseph Prince talks about in his book *Unmerited Favor*. It also was a real-life example of the practical benefits of letting go and letting God.

After returning from terminal leave, I began my career as a full-time realtor in February 2014. I had been told that, for planning purposes, I should be fully prepared to have no clients and no income from real estate for as long as six to 12 months. This was because I was building a "sales pipeline" from scratch, self-sourcing all my own client leads (as opposed to being given leads by an established agent as a part of their team). Within two weeks, though, I had my first clients. Within another two months, we had put an offer on a property they really wanted. This was in April 2014, in a red-hot seller's market in the D.C. area. This particular listing had multiple offers within the first couple days of hitting the market.

In these situations, many times sellers will call for what's called a "best and final" offer from all interested parties due to the high level of demand. Basically, this means that if we wanted to have any shot at getting this property, we couldn't lowball the sellers but had to give our very best offer the first time. Sure enough, the listing called for best and final offers to be submitted after only six days on the market, so we knew we had to put in the best possible offer the very first time if we wanted to have a chance of getting this property.

My clients and I had some concerns because several factors made us less competitive than other potential buyers. For one, we were using a VA loan, which has a few extra requirements and hoops sellers have to jump through, costs them more money, and can typically cause a longer timeline for closing. The sellers were on a tight timeline. Also, we were taking advantage of the VA loan's 100% financing option, using no money down. Finally, there were multiple "contingencies" that can complicate and add requirements for the seller. The first one is the financing contingency, meaning that if the loan falls through for any reason, the deal is off. Secondly, there was the home inspection contingency as well as a radon (poisonous gas) inspection contingency.

When we walked through the house for the first time, my clients (who are also believers) and I held hands together and prayed the following prayer: "God, if this house is *not* Your best, please close the door and take away the desire and the peace for moving forward in purchasing it. If, however, this house is meant to be Your blessing, then we ask that you allow our offer to be accepted, not *because* of but *despite* circumstances, so there will be no doubt in anyone's mind whatsoever that You and *only* You are the reason for it. We thank you in advance for your best for us. Amen."

The listing price of this property was $440,000, but we knew we were going to have to come in above asking price to be competitive. My clients initially decided to offer $445,500, but for various reasons, we increased this by $500 for an offer price of $446,000. Later, I felt led by the Holy Spirit to do a "Jericho walk" around the house: circling it seven times, praying in tongues, physically laying my hands on it, and declaring scriptures out loud.

The day after we put in the offering, the listing agent called and told me that we had a "verbal contract" on the house and to expect the official paperwork later that day! She then went on to tell me that she had never seen a deal quite like this in her 30 years of experience in the industry. She told me one of the other offers was *all cash* and required *no contingencies*! There is no earthly reason the sellers should have gone with our offer over that one. Furthermore, she said that we had beat that all-cash offer by **exactly $500**! Had we not changed our original offer of $445,500, we would have been exactly the same dollar value as the cash offer.

> *If this house is meant to be Your blessing, then we ask that you allow our offer to be accepted...so there will be no doubt...that You and only You are the reason for it.*

She told me how savvy I was in structuring this deal and that she could not believe this was my first-ever contract as a realtor. I appreciated her kind words and definitely always try to conduct myself with a spirit of excellence, working as to the

Lord. But I told her that this was undeniably the favor and provision of God. I described to her how I had done the Jericho march around the house and prayed with my clients.

We ended up closing the deal 21 days later, in what is about half the time such a deal would usually take. After hearing all the details of this transaction, several of the veteran agents at my brokerage asked me, "Seriously, though, *why did they accept your offer!?*" I responded, "so I could share this testimony with you of God's goodness and provision!" From planning on having no clients or income for six to 12 months to getting my first clients within two weeks and then a *totally miraculous* first sale within another two months, this was a pretty amazing debut as a realtor. But even more amazing than the results is the fact that, just as we prayed for, God clearly and undeniably gets the credit for it.

My second home sale as a realtor was also very blessed. At this time, I was living in that room my friend offered me in his home for $500 per month. I was riding the momentum from my first sale and hustling to generate more leads for my business. One day a few months after that first sale, my mom called and encouraged me to consider taking a week or two of vacation to visit my sister. My sister had been in South America for about nine months and was about to come home after traveling to Machu Picchu in Peru. Apparently, she needed some encouragement, so my mom thought it might be a nice ministry opportunity for me to visit her and enjoy a vacation at one of the seven wonders of the world.

At first, I wouldn't even consider it. I felt like I needed to stay focused on building my business. I was concerned this vacation would hurt my ability to generate leads and cause me to miss opportunities. My mom was fairly persistent about it, though, so I stayed just *barely* open-minded enough to ask the Holy Spirit if this was something I should do. For that to happen, He would have to make it so supernaturally obvious that I couldn't possibly miss it (even though I wanted to). When I mentioned this to Jenny (the wife of my friend John, who had invited me to stay in his house), she very strongly encouraged me to take the vacation.

This surprised me and made me just a little more open to the idea. I told God that if I could find astoundingly low last-second prices for airline tickets and not pay out of pocket for any of the necessary clothes and gear I'd need for the trip, I'd seriously consider it. Almost to my chagrin, there were indeed last-minute ticket prices for cheaper than I would have believed. I was also able to borrow about $1,500 worth of clothes, gear, and a backpack from the family I lived with. Hmmm… despite myself, I now had no more excuses for not taking the trip. I felt guilty for taking another extravagant overseas vacation when I had just taken one three months before while I was on terminal leave. I felt like this was the season I needed to be "on my grind" in building my business.

Psalm 23:2 says, "He *makes* me lie down in green pastures" (my emphasis). It seemed like this was what God was trying to get me to do right now. So, I submitted

> *God had been working while I was resting.*

to the guidance of the Holy Spirit and *made* myself take this two-week vacation. I had a wonderful vacation seeing Machu Picchu, and more importantly, I had some breakthrough moments and conversations with my sister. I was grateful for this new lifestyle of self-employed freedom that allowed me to do something this spontaneous, something I never could have done in the Navy on such short notice.

It turned out that God had been working while I was resting on this vacation. When I got back, Jenny remarked that "my energy looked different" from having taken this vacation. They weren't planning on selling their house for several years, but for no other apparent reason, she committed right that moment to use me as her listing agent whenever they did! I was taken completely off guard by this but was obviously thrilled. "What just happened?!" I thought to myself. This was a high-dollar house in an upscale area, and they had been planning on listing it with the realtor who helped them buy it several years before. She was an extremely successful realtor who had been in the business for decades and dominated listings in that area. I had less than six months and one sale under my belt. It's very unusual to get a listing like that as a brand-new realtor. Nevertheless, she assured me: "You're our guy now, Ryan."

Several months later in September 2014, they unexpectedly felt an unction from the Holy Spirit that it was time to sell. This home became my first listing, which sold within six days on the market for $825,000! The buyers appeared to be exactly the kind of family we'd all been praying for, which was very important to my clients. Not bad, for a first listing. Taking that vacation did not cause me to miss business opportunities, as I had originally feared. In fact, it brought business *to* me in such a way that cannot rationally be explained. That *two-week vacation* generated the largest paycheck I've ever had to this day! If that doesn't demand a supernatural explanation, I don't know what does...

In Matthew 11:28–30 (MSG, my emphasis), Jesus says something so refreshing:

> Are you tired? Worn out? Burned out on religion? Come to me. Get away with me and you'll recover your life. I'll show you how to take a real rest. **Walk with me and work with me—watch how I do it. Learn the unforced rhythms of grace.** I won't lay anything heavy or ill-fitting on you. Keep company with me and you'll learn to live freely and lightly.

By submitting to the conviction of the Holy Spirit *"making me lie down in green pastures,"* I was trained how to greatly prosper *Jesus'* way: by tapping into the "unforced rhythms of grace."

After this listing, I closed a few more transactions, and my sales pipeline started filling up with in-bound leads from referrals. In April 2015, I attended a real estate sales conference hosted by Brian Buffini. You may recall Brian as the co-author of *Work by Referral*, the book that was a major influence on me becoming a realtor. At this conference, he was talking about the difference between willpower and "why power." He described how willpower alone would always fail us when things got tough in business. He said that we needed a deep and personally meaningful reason *why* we're doing what we do. He then asked the audience a question: "Is your *why* strong enough to be in the real estate business?"

If I was being totally honest with myself, I doubted my *why* as a realtor was strong enough. I liked many aspects of the business: the flexibility and freedom of being self-employed, the creativity to build one's business around one's interests and relationships, unlimited income potential, and the self-development required to succeed in the business. But those weren't enough for me in and of themselves. What I realized in that moment, though, was that what I really wanted was *his* job! I wanted to be exactly where he was and doing what he was doing right there on that stage: employing skillful communication to inspire people to become the most successful and fulfilled people they possibly could be.

> *I was trained how to greatly prosper Jesus' way: by tapping into the "unforced rhythms of grace."*

I realized I was called primarily to the field of *inspirational communication and personal development*. In a state of shock from the realization that my *why* as a realtor wasn't strong enough, I left the conference building to go on a walk around the block and clear my head. As I was walking, I talked to God about my confusion and asked for His opinion of the situation. I was convinced of the fact that He was the One who had improbably led me into the real estate business in the first place and felt like I was barely even established in that field, much less ready to move on. Surely, He had a purpose and plan in bringing me to this point, a critically important assignment that I needed to carry out. What He said then stopped me in my tracks.

He lovingly and matter-of-factly said something that made no sense to me at all: *Ryan, I don't need you to do anything.* Come again?!? *I don't need you to do anything for Me. The universe does not rise and fall on whether or not you step into your God-given assignment.* This was both immensely relieving and shockingly humbling. I had made so much of the importance— nay, the *necessity*—of my stepping into my divine purpose and assignment. While I absolutely still believe this is an opportunity to be used by God in a life-giving and fulfilling way to bless others and demonstrate His goodness and faithfulness, I was losing perspective of the primary purpose of my existence: to know God and be known by Him, to love Him and be loved *by* Him.

> *I was more important to Him as a son than I ever would or could be as a servant.*

He was not interested in me being a cog in the wheel of His grand designs for the universe. Like Jesus said about how the sabbath was made for *man* and *not* man for the Sabbath, I believe my Father was telling me in a provocative way that I was more important to Him as a **son** than I ever would or could be as a **servant**. Trust me when I tell you that this is a revelation that is still very much in process for me, but it was an important paradigm shift that really caused me to reevaluate my perspective at the time. In fact, it would very shortly lead to yet another major and unexpected decision.

PRACTICAL REFLECTION AND PERSONAL APPLICATION

Are you striving to make things happen in your own effort and strength? Are you tired? Worn out? Burned out on religion? Take Jesus up on His offer in Matthew 11:28–30 to get away with Him: walk with Him, work with Him, watch how *He* does it. He will teach you the "unforced rhythms of grace." As I can attest, this will give you more peace and rest in your life that will also bring practical, bottom-line results.

CHAPTER 9

WHAT IS IN
YOUR HEART?

I was still reeling from the revelation that God didn't seem all that concerned about whether or not I stayed in the real estate industry. I decided I needed to get away from all distractions and busyness, take some time of personal reflection with the Lord, and seek His direction on whether or not to continue as a realtor. Getting away from the hustle and bustle is not a trivial matter to a 21st-century realtor living in the frenetic pace of our nation's capital, constantly tethered to a phone and electronic devices 24/7. But despite starting to see more of the fruit from my labor in building my business, there was no denying the growing disquiet and inexplicable lack of peace within my soul.

I spent four days at a monastery in the outskirts of the Northern Virginia area that facilitates retreats of complete personal silence "off the grid" with no electronics. This monastery had a lot of acreage in a peaceful and quiet area in the countryside. As I drove farther away from the city, slowly but surely, I began to unwind from the unrelenting and insidiously fast-paced rhythms of the city. One of my friends refers to this as the "D.C. plastic wrap:" a suffocating heaviness in the atmosphere within about a one-hour radius from downtown D.C. It's a spiritual and even physical sensation one sometimes feels.

Farther into the beautifully quiet and serene countryside, a peaceful calm and slower rhythm began to develop internally. Eventually, all that could be heard was the steady background hum of buzzing insects and occasional wind through the trees. More than anything, it was the conspicuous quiet and stillness that arrested my soul. This was sorely needed and hugely helpful for me to be able to tap into those "unforced rhythms of grace" so I could hear clearly from the Holy Spirit.

I had a modest but clean and private room. There were common areas in the chapel and various locations around the property. On rare occasions, I'd see other retreatants walking around the building or outside on the property. Generally, though, everyone made themselves pretty scarce. No talking was allowed in order to facilitate the monastery as a haven of personal silence, prayer, and reflection. I was grateful for this, as I imagine others were as well. As I journaled and read the Word in this peaceful and restful environment, I more clearly heard God's still, small voice speaking to me.

Within the first 24 hours, I sensed I may have heard God releasing me from real estate, telling me to wait on Him indefinitely for the next steps to effortlessly present themselves to me. It took the next 72 hours for Him to convince me it was actually *His* voice I had heard and not the devil or my own flesh leading me astray. In a misguided belief that I needed to "keep my hand to the plow" and continue to be faithful where God had me, even if it didn't feel life-giving or enjoyable, I was feeling really guilty about the thought of doing something else that was more easy, natural, and enjoyable. **Most of my life, I related to God as "the God who requires difficult things of me because it will be good for me in the end."**

God had to convince me that *His* will and path for me are a natural fit, reminding me of the revelation I had when reading the book *StrengthsFinder* by Tom Rath. God began to show me that the DOD spirit was, once again, actually getting in the way of all He had for me. He told me that He really is a good Father and has good things in store for me; that I was a *son*, not a clone or a servant. He asked me the question, "How does a good earthly father raise his son?" After some objective and honest reflection, I came to the following answer: by instructing him on the basis of an unshakable foundation of unconditional love, principles, character, discipline, demonstrated instruction, and **progressive freedom to make his own choices and ultimately live out his own life.**

These choices and this life will hopefully reflect the values and goodness of how he was raised based on general principles but manifested in a way that is unique to the individual son, distinct from any other person or path. Good fathers raise good sons by drawing out and cultivating their son's (or daughter's) unique gifts, strengths, and talents, thus empowering them to live out the unique dreams, passions, and ultimate purpose that has been put inside of them.

A proverb came to my mind at this point: "Raise up a child in the way *he* should go and he will not depart from it" (Proverbs 22:6, emphasis mine). The Lord was highlighting to me in this verse that the way in which the child should go was unique to the child and was merely facilitated (as opposed to determined) by the earthly father. The Lord said to me, *The only way I can enable you so that you "do not depart from it" is to empower and release you to live out the desires of your heart, which I've designed within you to walk in before the foundations of the earth were laid.*

This reminded me of a verse I'd heard many times before but was now highlighted to me in a new way: "For we are His workmanship, created in Christ Jesus for good works, which God prepared beforehand that we should walk in them" (Ephesians

2:10). All of this seemed to be progressively revealing to me that this desire in my heart to leave my real estate career to pursue something more in line with my inherent dreams and desires (which still weren't totally clear) might actually be from God and not just me. However, it was still hard for me to know which thoughts were mine, which were from God, and which were from the enemy (that great deceiver).

I asked for the "mind of Christ" right then, and Jesus gave me some scriptures that came unbidden to my mind: "My sheep hear Me and know My voice, and the voice of another they will not follow" (John 10:4–5). "Without faith it is impossible to please God, for those who come to Him must believe that He exists and that He rewards those that earnestly seek Him" (Hebrews 11:6). In response to this last scripture, the Father clearly said to me:

> *Have you not earnestly sought Me? Have you not set this time apart as holy, to hear from Me and commune with Me? Am I so cold and unwilling to meet you that I would not readily present Myself to you when you seek Me? Have I not said, "Draw near to God, and He will draw near to you?" Does the ease with which you now hear Me startle you, even after all these years? What good father would remain so aloof from his very own son? It breaks my heart that you think and feel this way, my son. Don't you yet know how loved you are in my sight? I am not an onerous taskmaster. I love you, I'm proud of you, and I am for you, Ryan; this is the mind of Christ for you.*

Yet, my own mind—and no doubt the enemy—were working against me to keep me from embracing this new freedom my Father was trying to lead me into. I still feared that all of these verses and God's supposed direct words to me were still just my own mind and flesh trying to justify going my own way with some kind of self-serving deception. It was then that I had another profound realization: **Fear of being deceived** was *itself* **the deception!**

I have to admit that our enemy is indeed a cunning adversary... however, his lies and deception don't stand a chance against the life-giving Truth of God! God then said to me:

> *"I will instruct you and teach you in the way in which you should go; I will counsel you with my eye upon you"* (Psalm 32:8). *"Whether you turn to the right or to the left, your ears will hear a voice behind you, saying, 'This is the way; walk in it.'"* (Isaiah 30:21). *"The steadfast of mind [I] will keep in perfect peace, because [you] trust in [Me]"* (Isaiah 26:3). *"[I], who did not spare [My] own Son, but delivered Him over for [you] all, how will [I] not also freely give you all things?"* (Romans 8:32).

I then felt God prompt me to read a book by Joseph Prince I was in the middle of at the time, called *Unmerited Favor.* Almost right away, I read a passage from page 158 that said, "Find your identity in Him [Jesus], and He will give you a new beginning, a fresh start, and a new page to begin an exciting life with Him! Now, with Jesus by your side, you can begin your new life of unmerited favor and success!" Given the context of considering a major transition into something brand-new, this absolutely jumped off the page to me!

However, the clincher for me came on page 165: **"For those of you who want to serve the Lord, but don't know where to start, just ask yourself what is in your heart...** As a new covenant believer, that's how your Father leads you. *He puts His laws in your mind and writes them on you heart"* [emphases mine]. That's when Prince quoted Philippians 2:13: "For it is God who is at work in you, both to will and to work according to His good purpose." That was it for me, the coup de gras. After reading that verse, which so timely and relevantly spoke to my exact situation and concerns, it was too much to deny. I knew that *God* was indeed the One speaking to me about truly following the desires in my heart. For me, this meant leaving real estate and pursuing something else.

After God had clearly released me from my job in real estate, the next logical question was: "What's next?" I was clear about what I was supposed to leave but had no idea of where I'd be going. Like Joshua and Caleb, I needed courage and faith to step into this next stage of my life as I crossed into the Promised Land He was leading me to. I didn't want to be like all the other Israelites of Joshua and Caleb's generation who died out in the wilderness without ever entering into the promises of God because of their unbelief and doubt. Though I had no idea what was next, I wanted to be open to whatever God had for me. I heard the Lord say to me, *This is a difficult but good and exciting thing for you. This is the battle I have called you to. I work in a pattern of good for those who love me and are called according to My purposes. Where your will intersects mine is the area of greatest ease and excitement for you. It may be well with your soul to choose what is in your heart already.*

At this point, I felt the way I imagine Abraham (named Abram at the time) must have felt when, "The LORD had said to Abram, 'Go from your country, your people, and your father's household to the land I *will* **[future tense]** show you'" (Genesis 12:1, my emphasis). God asked Abram to pack up and leave the area he was familiar with, where everyone he knew lived, and where he had been prospering... without any idea of where he was going next. As a man of considerable wealth with an extensive family, I can only imagine the logistics of organizing everyone, packing up, and getting it on the road. I also wonder what his conversations must have been like with his friends and family members about *why* they were all moving ("God told me to") and where they were moving to ("Oh, I don't know that yet...").

There seems to be a fine line between faith and foolishness many times in the Bible as well as modern-day life. I think of the conversations Joshua must have had with his military commanders when he told them the battle plan was to march around a heavily fortified city for seven days blowing trumpets and yelling. Or Gideon voluntarily reducing the number of

God was showing me the sacredness of rest as He went to work on my behalf.

his fighting men from 32,000 down to 300 before a major battle with an army that impossibly outnumbered them. In all of these examples, though, no matter how foolish the plans seemed to be from a human perspective, time and time again the wisest choice was to trust and obey the Lord. The victories that followed such incredible acts of faith undeniably demonstrated God's power, love, provision, and goodness in such a radical way.

The hardest thing for me at this point was to realize that **there was nothing I had to do in order to bring about the Lord's blessing for this next step in my life. My only part was to rest, wait, and trust.** This was hard to accept because to my natural senses, it felt like laziness, foolishness, irrationality, and ungodliness to sit around waiting, doing no work whatsoever. As a self-employed realtor working solely on a commission basis, the income I earned was exclusively the result of sales I personally closed. So, I was used to hustling pretty hard. My tendency is almost always to think I need to be doing more, trying and working harder.

However, God was showing me the sacredness of rest as *He* went to work on my behalf. This was a very practical, personal picture of this new understanding of grace: defined not so much by forgiveness but as the cessation of my own human striving, effort, work, and toil. It was all about receiving the *finished* work Jesus already accomplished on my behalf, which doesn't end at being born again. It is a lifelong, ongoing process of simply receiving *all* of God's benefits by faith and belief as opposed to a merit system, a system I was all too familiar with.

I felt God say to me: *As you continue to wait on Me only, you will be blessed. I'm preparing to take you on a journey of faith with Me, son; I will never leave you nor forsake you. I, the Lord Your God, go before you into the good land that I have promised you. Therefore, be strong and courageous, knowing that I will uphold you by My righteous right hand and tell you where to go, saying, "This is the Way, walk in Him"* [Jesus is the Way, the Truth, and the Life].

I still couldn't believe this was actually happening. Inside of me was such a sense of hope, excitement, and expectancy; it all just seemed too good to be true. Then I remembered something my pastor once said: "If it seems too good to be true, it's God." God seemed to be affirming to me that was true in this instance. He said: ***Expect** **things to resonate in your heart; that is My signature and My calling card in your heart, upon which I seal the signet ring of Hope and Expectancy.*** I went to bed that second night in the monastery with a full heart.

PERSONAL REFLECTION AND PRACTICAL APPLICATION

What is in *your* heart? If you are feeling drained and unfulfilled, take some time away from the busyness and demands of life to hear from God clearly. You may want to consider going away on a retreat in a different area. Regardless of the location, cut yourself off from the distractions of the world for long enough to settle into the stillness and peace where you can hear God speak to you clearly and powerfully. Journaling is an excellent tool for this. This literally changed my life, and it can for you as well.

CHAPTER 10

INVESTING IN REST

The next morning, I was in a panic. The magnitude of what I was considering overwhelmed me. I devolved into doubting I was really hearing from God and that I was making a terrible decision. But Jesus assured me of His words in Matthew 11:28: *My yoke is easy, and My burden is light.* I was reminded of a prophetic word I had recently received from a very trustworthy and powerful man of God, who said, "This is a hard thing: God wants you to trust Him." Part of trusting God is trusting the desires He places within our hearts and the Holy Spirit's inner witness of peace and joy that results from those desires.

Journaling is a powerful way for me to get in touch with the God-given desires of my heart and hear God's voice. As I journaled, I heard God continue speaking to me:

The more aware you are of My intimate, minute involvement in all aspects of your life, the more peace, faith, trust, and joy you will experience. As you apprehend My presence more and more with your spiritual faculties, I will become more real and personal than you've ever known. **Be willing to trust your impressions, impulses, and sensations in your heart.** *It is only by allowing yourself the* *freedom to fully follow your heart that you will learn what is from Me and what is not; you learn this from both your failures as well as your successes.*

Hearing these life-giving words spoken into my spirit reassured me as peace displaced the panic I woke up with. It gave me freedom to look at things as a "prayerful experiment." I didn't have to get it perfectly right. God was giving me the grace to fail as well as to succeed, knowing it would all work together to deepen my trust and relationship with Him. If anything, the only stern warning was not to do anything in my own effort or strength any more: *Man's tendency is to go ahead of My Word and do things in his own timing under his own power.* **Don't you know that I can accomplish in a moment what you could never accomplish in a lifetime?** *Wait on Me; abide in Me, Ryan. I will never fail you; that is My promise to you.*

Anything of significance that ever happens in the Kingdom of God is done through faith. When I say faith, I'm not talking about the legalism masquerading as faith that is so prevalent in certain Christian circles. Faith is not something we can generate or work up in our own human effort. Therefore, even faith is something we can only receive through God's grace. It is simply believing, resting in, and appropriating all that God has given us through His grace. **Grace is the whole package, from start to finish. Grace is what sets Christianity apart from every other religion.**

That's because every other religion invokes some form of "karma," which is really just the law: human performance to earn divine or cosmic blessing. Only Christianity says that *God* performed in order to bless *us*. This was done, once and for all, through the finished work of the cross in Jesus Christ. From a business perspective, you can think of grace as Christianity's "unique value proposition" or "competitive advantage" in the marketplace of performance-based religion. Hallelujah! What a good God we serve; He actually serves us! (Mark 10:45). Continuing this business analogy of God's offer—and *command*—for us to rest in His work (Hebrews 4), God gave me a "business proposition" at the monastery. He used this as an illustration to encourage me to trust Him completely in my transition season.

This is the scenario: I am the sole proprietor of my own business. I do all the work myself and keep 100% of the profits ($100,000 yearly). I do one deal with a guy named Jesus on a contract basis. This guy Jesus does such a good job that I decide to do a few more contracts with Him for larger deals each time. Because of Him, the business does well enough that I decide to form a new corporation with Him as a minority shareholder. Whatever He does prospers so much that I then make Him a 50/50 partner and eventually Chairman of the Board. I go from Chairman to Board Member to a humble minority shareholder. The corporation prospers in direct proportion to how much He increases and I decrease.

But that's totally fine with me because I'm just sitting back and collecting ever-larger dividends at the same time as the valuation of the company grows exponentially under His leadership and guidance. I'm no longer overseeing anything or doing any of the work myself; I'm just sitting back and collecting checks as *His* wisdom, guidance, personnel decisions, and strategy increase the company's market share and profitability. The question God posed was this: **"Would you rather be 100% owner of a $100,000 company, or a 1% minority stakeholder of a $500 billion corporation I'm running?"** (In case you're wondering, 1% of $500 billion is $5 billion).

That's what happens as we increasingly give God control of our lives. Who cares if you're not running the show, as long as the bottom line goes up? As a financial investor, the *best* investments I always look for are the ones that produce *passive income* (regular income I don't have to work for or earn). Even the IRS recognizes the superiority of passive income over "earned" income! Earned income (from *wages* paid to you as an employee) is generally taxed at a much higher rate than the passive income or capital gains generated by investments.

Even when it comes to the US tax code, you could say that "earning" it is *more* "taxing" and *less* profitable than simply receiving it. Anyone who has built a large amount of wealth has done so not primarily through earning their pay as wages but rather through the acquisition of tax-efficient assets and investments. Instead of working for money, money is working for *them*.

The idea behind an investment is that one must first give something up (called the "principal") in order to later receive back more than what was initially invested (called the "return"). A really good investment opportunity will protect the original principal amount, yield the investor a present return in the form of a steady income stream, and also provide a very large future payoff in the form of appreciation of asset value that is many multiples of the principal. An investment that most people would say is too good to be true is one that is absolutely guaranteed.

However, Jesus described just such an investment that is available to all of us (Mark 10:29–31 MSG): "Mark my words, no one who sacrifices house, brothers, sisters, mother, father, children, land—whatever—because of me and the Message will lose out. They'll get it all back, but multiplied many times in homes, brothers, sisters, mothers, children, and land—but also in troubles. And then the bonus of eternal life!" **In this** remarkable passage of scripture, Jesus starts by giving a <u>personal guarantee</u> of investment success. He then promises the present benefit of what we will receive back in this life and ends with the "bonus" of the future payoff of eternal life. Building on what I mentioned earlier, I once sensed the Holy Spirit say, "When something sounds too good to be true, it's virtually certain to be one of two things: the lies of men or the Truth of God."

The "principal," which I believe we must all give up as our "investment" in rest to yield the return of God's highest and best for our lives, can most simply and essentially be reduced to this: **self-effort**. We have an invitation to trust God by making the counterintuitive and countercultural decision to give up our own human wisdom and strength in exchange for God's wisdom and strength. This is in accordance with 1 Corinthians 1:25 (NIV): "Because the foolishness of God is wiser than human wisdom, and the weakness of God is stronger than human strength." By doing so, we avoid the hard work of toil, striving, anxiety, and limited human ability.

When I removed myself from my busy life and came to this very restful place of stillness and silence at the monastery, I became more aware of and sensitive to my own self-effort and striving.

In any truthful financial investment prospectus, you will always see some iteration of the following caveat: "Past performance is not a guarantee of future results." With the true Gospel of Grace, though, once again, this is not true. Jesus' perfect performance in His life absolutely guarantees our future and our results with returns as high as 30, 60, or even 100 times (Matthew 13:8)! The Word of God, and perhaps more importantly, the lives of those it has transformed with the Gospel, have the metrics and case studies to back up this seemingly preposterous claim.

It was only when I removed myself from my busy life and came to this very restful place of stillness and silence at the monastery that I became more aware of and sensitive to my own self-effort and striving. As I was preparing to leave this place and re-enter my life back home on an indefinite sabbatical, God spoke some final words of wisdom and encouragement to me:

> *When you get back, just do what comes naturally to you: connect with people, journal, pray, read My Word, and plan your dream. As you effortlessly and instinctively run the script of what I've put inside you, it will intersect you with the plans and desires I've put in your heart. I have called you into a season of rest. It is only **from this rest** in your body, soul, and spirit that you will be **energized to action**. I'm breaking you of all striving and performance so that you will be completely dependent on Me for your sole sufficiency and provision. You are Mine and Mine alone. You're going back to a life that is free and full of promise. **Enter into My rest!***

PERSONAL REFLECTION AND PRACTICAL APPLICATION

Invest in rest by giving up all self-effort. Ask the Holy Spirit for a life-altering revelation of God's all-encompassing grace, and He will teach you the superior method of receiving instead of earning. Allow yourself to be stretched—maybe even uncomfortable—in walking by faith, as opposed to walking by sight (human thinking and reasoning). Make God the "Chairman of the Board" in your life, and you will receive the dividends of *His* work and blessings. You will prosper and be blessed to the extent that He takes a greater role in your life. Trust that from a place of rest, you *will* be energized to action by God's Spirit working through you.

CHAPTER 11

GO WEST, YOUNG MAN

After returning from the monastery, I did as God directed and waited on Him for whatever He had next. "Waiting" on God is not to be confused with passivity or lack of intentionality. I was very actively praying, reading the Word, and exercising my faith to remain at rest. This went totally against the grain of my habits, training, and experiences. I was very used to "doing," so I had to force myself to settle into a new routine of listening quietly to God and adjust to a new rhythm. Mind renewal is not always an easy thing when you're put in a position that challenges you to go against deeply ingrained, lifelong thinking and habit patterns. But I would soon find that my waiting was not in vain.

A few weeks before I had left for the monastery, a friend named Dan had an amazing experience with a veteran organization that ministers to other veterans. He strongly encouraged me to attend one of their retreats, and he put me in touch with someone from the ministry. At the time, there was a minimum six-month waiting list for the next retreat. However, shortly

> *"Waiting" on God is not to be confused with passivity or lack of intentionality.*

after returning from the monastery, I got an unexpected call from someone at the ministry. He said a last-minute spot had opened up for me to attend the next retreat, which was only a few weeks away! It definitely seemed more than coincidental to me, being that I was waiting on a word from God that He had something for me if I would just make myself available to Him. I booked the flight and confirmed my spot with the ministry.

I had a real estate deal from a few months before that was scheduled to close while I was gone. By this point, pretty much everything that needed to be done was taken care of, all the paperwork was in order, and it was just a matter of time, so I coordinated with another realtor from my firm to physically attend the settlement in my stead. With that taken care of, I was ready to go.

Part of the preparation for the retreat was to read a book by John Eldredge called *Wild at Heart*. In this book, the author talks about reclaiming the masculine soul God created in men and "living from our deep heart," as he called it. One of the lines quoted in the book (originally from Howard Thurman) really spoke to me and seemed to confirm what God had been telling me at the monastery: "Don't ask what the world needs. Ask yourself what makes you come alive, and go do. Because what the world needs are people who have come alive."

That confirmed to me what God had been telling me at the monastery and during my time of rest. It gave me a greater sense of freedom and permission to act out of the deep longings and passions I was now realizing *God* had put there. I allowed myself to stop living life from a well-meaning but misdirected notion of doing what I thought was "the right thing" if it didn't create within me a sense of passion, joy, and adventure and make me come alive at the deepest level of my heart. I was now committing to myself, God, and others—especially during this transition time of my life—to make decisions based on what made me come alive and not what I felt an obligation toward, to "lean in" to the adventure of walking by faith God had me on.

On a related note, one of the things that was really emphasized to us at the retreat was living from our hearts and not our heads. My natural tendency for most of my life, especially when making seemingly important decisions, was to be very cerebral and to intellectualize things. Those of us on the retreat all made a commitment on the last day to live more from our hearts and less from our heads. This commitment was immediately tested the very minute the retreat was over.

One of the men I had connected with on the retreat was going through a really tough time in his marriage. He was planning on staying a few extra days to help the ranch manager fix up a cabin on the retreat property. He asked me that last night if I would stay and help him do this. He could use some help with the manual labor, but mainly, he just needed some godly fellowship as he processed everything we had just experienced in light of navigating his marriage challenges. I was inclined to say yes, but told him I needed to make sure everything was going smoothly back home. Once we were allowed to turn our cell phones back on, I got an email from the realtor who I had coordinated with earlier to facilitate the closing in my absence.

Apparently the closing for that day hit a snag, and it sounded as if the deal was in jeopardy of falling through. She recommended I come back immediately to deal with the situation. I instinctively reverted back into striving, performance, and "get stuff done" mode. I was seriously tempted to fly back to D.C. to handle this work crisis. I had been working that deal for many months, and many thousands of dollars were at stake. Furthermore, I had referred out most of my other clients and transactions and didn't have much left in the pipeline by now. But in light of what I had just committed to about living from my deep heart's desires and not my head, I brought this issue to the retreat facilitators. Without hesitation, the first thing they asked was, "What does your heart say?"

Ugh, why did they have to ask me *that*?! It didn't take me more than a moment to admit that my heart was telling me to stay those few extra days with my friend and trust God with the real estate deal. So I made the decision, changed my flight, and committed to stay with my friend. The more I thought about it, I realized that even if I got back to D.C. that day, there was nothing I could do about it anyway. It would be whatever it would be, but my heart was set, and I was going to trust my heart even if it didn't make sense to my head, which was screaming at me to go home and do "the responsible thing."

In Isaiah 30:15–16 (NIV), the Lord says, "In returning and rest you shall be saved; in quietness and confidence shall be your strength." Our flesh wants to do things our way, but God's invitation to rest means trusting His way. Striving to accomplish tasks is a very real temptation, especially when you're in a profession that requires generating your own income.

In this decision, I had to repent and return to rest even though it involved risking my professional reputation and commission check. But those fears were born of my flesh. That wasn't coming from a place of faith, trust, and rest in God. And to be able to experience God's best, I had to once again repent and be willing to think and act differently than I had in the past. I was living the adventure with God now, and I was learning at a deeper level that one of the things that makes

> *"In returning and rest you shall be saved; in quietness and confidence shall be your strength."*

adventure so exhilarating is the sense of risk and uncertainty associated with spontaneity and taking the limits off. I refused to be shackled by the security of predictability.

Sure enough, the deal ended up closing within a few days, and everything worked out just fine. More importantly, I had learned to live less transactionally and more relationally both with God as well as my fellow man. I was experiencing and submitting to a decision-making process based on a Kingdom value system and heavenly priorities instead of worldly thinking. As the Apostle Paul says:

> So here's what I want you to do, God helping you: Take your everyday, ordinary life—your sleeping, eating, ***going-to-work***, and walking-around life—and place it before God as an offering. Embracing what God does for you is the best thing you can do for him. Don't become so well-adjusted to your culture that you fit into it without even thinking. Instead, fix your attention on God. You'll be changed from the inside out. Readily recognize what he wants from you, and quickly respond to it. Unlike the culture around you, always dragging you down to its level of immaturity, God brings the best out of you, develops well-formed maturity in you" (Romans 12:1–2, MSG; author's emphasis).

In short, I was learning a better way of doing life and business by putting my money where my mouth was in trusting God to live from the heart, walk by faith, and invest in rest when the rubber met the road.

"Your faith is never really tested until you're tempted to doubt."

As Pastor Duane Sheriff says, "Your faith is never really tested until you're tempted to doubt." Another person also made the observation that you're not going to grow stronger in the physical realm until you go out of your comfort zone and lift heavier weights. Your muscles have to be torn and broken down by being pushed beyond their current limitations, and only then can they be rebuilt stronger. So it is with our faith if we want to get "jacked," or stronger, in the spiritual realm. As Proverbs 3:5–6 (AMP) says, "Trust in and rely confidently on the LORD with all your heart and do not rely on your own insight or understanding. In all your ways know and acknowledge and recognize Him, And He will make your paths straight and smooth [removing obstacles that block your way]."

As a result of doing what the Holy Spirit had put in my heart despite my inclination to do the opposite, I was richly rewarded in the natural realm. These extra days with my friend were a huge blessing for us both as we got closer to God and each other in the days following the retreat. As I was journaling those several days, I also felt that God was building expectancy in my heart for something else of significance He had in store for that impromptu extension of my time there. I had the sense that I would not leave Colorado without something developing that would change the direction of my life and lead to practical next steps as I waited on God for whatever He had in store.

One day as my friend and I were working on the cabin, a man named Kenny came by to see what we were doing and introduce himself to us. He was a member of the Board of Directors for the foundation that owned the ranch and had also previously attended the retreat we had just experienced. As fellow brothers in Christ who had all gone through this powerful experience, an instant bond was created. As we began to talk more, I discovered Kenny was a successful serial entrepreneur who was working on a new business idea.

After he learned about my military experience as well as my business background and education, he was intrigued about me. When I told him about my recent journey at the monastery and how I was trusting and waiting on God for the next steps, he mentioned that he was currently in the process of putting a core team together for this new company and would be interested in having someone like me on board. We briefly prayed together right there and decided to keep the matter in prayer and stay in touch after I got back to D.C. With this exciting possibility in mind, I had a great time for the rest of my trip and left with confirmation of the earlier sense I had: Staying those extra days after the retreat was not a coincidence—God had a plan and purpose in that.

Within a week of returning back home to Virginia, I got a couple of unexpected phone calls. The first was from Pete, the founder of the ministry who organized the retreats. He said he was looking to grow the ministry team that helped him facilitate the retreats and asked me if I would be willing to pray about possibly being a part of the team. I told him I thought this was a possible divine appointment and recounted to him my conversation with Kenny and the prospect of moving out there to work for him and the startup he was putting together.

Pete was not aware of the fact I had also been asked to potentially be part of that company, but he knew Kenny well and said "everything he touches turns to gold." He agreed that this may be a God thing and it was a great opportunity for me to consider. He then invited me to go on a ministry team retreat they were having in July at Lake Tahoe in a stunningly beautiful lakefront mansion! I gratefully accepted and was looking forward to getting to better know him, the team, and the ministry.

The other call I received that same week was from a man named Mark, who owned the ranch and the foundation that supported the ministry. He was an extremely wealthy and well-connected real estate investor whose name was mentioned several times at the retreat. He had heard my name come up several times between Doug (the man who had initially referred me to the ministry), as well as Kenny and Pete. He said he just wanted to introduce himself and get to know me in the near future. I was honored by his interest in me and told him I was planning to go back out to Colorado for an alumni event at the ministry in August.

By this point, it was becoming increasingly obvious to me that the Lord was indeed working behind the scenes on my behalf to orchestrate the details of the next season He was preparing me for. In a relatively short time after hearing from God at the monastery and making an illogical decision to quit my growing real estate business, I had been able to attend the retreat, been offered the possibility of an exciting job at a startup company, a spot on the ministry team, an amazing weekend in Lake Tahoe, and the chance to meet Mark at the alumni event.

In my time back home, I continued to seek the Lord and prepare my mind and heart for what was looking like an exciting adventure and major transition. I was spending most of my days essentially on an extended vacation, resting and dreaming with God through prayer, journaling, reading the Word, and talking to friends and family about all the recent developments. I was no longer actively building my business, but God was faithful to continue providing for me as I was able to refer almost all of my existing clients to other realtors and collect referral commissions from the sales.

After spending a beautiful long weekend in Lake Tahoe with the ministry team in July, I attended the alumni event back in the Vail Valley in August. I had a running dialogue with Kenny about working for him but nothing firm yet. He invited me to stay at his amazingly beautiful house during the alumni event and even let me drive his BMW convertible for the week or so I was there! However, after the first couple nights, he had to leave unexpectedly, so I would need another place to stay. At first, I was a little apprehensive since housing is extremely expensive and difficult to find in the Vail Valley, especially this weekend when a lot of hotels were booked in the area because of the alumni event.

However, God made provision once again. Kenny was good friends with Mark (the wealthy real estate investor who had called me to introduce himself a few months earlier) and arranged for me to stay at his house for the remainder of my stay. I finally met Mark in person and was welcomed into his home and his family. This home was beyond anything I had personally seen in my life. It was an enormous mansion on many acres of property in a very secluded and exclusive development in the Vail Valley. The views of the mountainside were absolutely stunning, especially at sunset.

Not being able to stay at Kenny's for the duration of my stay once again looked like a setback that in reality was a divine setup. After staying with Mark and his family for several days, I developed a quick rapport with them, and they offered to let me stay at their house if I were to move to Colorado. They were even going out of their way to find ways for me to be able to support myself working for the ranch and/or the foundation if the job offer didn't come through at the startup company.

I almost got the sense they'd be disappointed if I *didn't* move in with them. The room they offered me was an apartment in a separate wing of the mansion that I essentially had to myself. And the kicker was the rent: For all this, I would be paying only a $500 monthly tax-deductible donation to the foundation that supported the ministry! This was an area in which housing was extremely difficult to find at a time *USA Today* said it was the most unaffordable county in the country.

Even though (or perhaps *because*) I am a minimalist by nature and don't get too caught up in material things, God seemed to be giving me a "kiss on the cheek" with many material blessings and amazing opportunities as I followed the Holy Spirit in childlike faith and simplicity, one step at a time. This blessing wasn't because of how good or holy I was but simply because I was diligently seeking Him with my whole heart and willing to put my faith in Him. Hebrews 11:6 says, "Without faith it is impossible to please God, because anyone who comes to him must believe that he exists and that he rewards those who earnestly seek him." It certainly seemed like I was being rewarded for my faith.

God was also showing me that when we are willing to **listen for His voice and trust what He says, no matter how seemingly ridiculous and impossible**, He is "able to do immeasurably more than all we ask or imagine, according to his power that is at work within us" (Ephesians 3:20). However, the thing that blew my mind the most during this season was just how much God can bless us when we are seemingly doing "nothing," just resting and believing in His unmerited favor and goodness towards us.

PERSONAL REFLECTION AND PRACTICAL APPLICATION

Are there any ways in which you're trusting your own understanding instead of the Lord? This could be for your job, business, finances, a move, or other major life decisions. Ask the Holy Spirit to speak to you about this as you meditate on Proverbs 3:5–6, which says, "Trust in the Lord with all your heart, and lean not on your own understanding; in all your ways acknowledge Him, and He shall direct your paths." Isaiah 30:15–16 is another great verse to ponder and journal about. Fight the temptation to "ride on swift horses" by toiling and striving in your flesh to accomplish what God can do on your behalf.

CHAPTER 12

HIGH ON THE MOUNTAINTOP

I moved to the Vail Valley in late September 2015. One critical aspect of this season was the "negotiation"—or lack thereof—concerning my compensation package as I joined Kenny's business startup team. I had done a lot of research online for compensation packages of comparable companies for people with comparable experience and skill sets that I had. I ran the numbers and budgets for what I would be willing to ask him for as well as the minimum I would be willing to accept for my pay and benefits. However, after exhaustive analysis and consideration, on the day that I was scheduled to enter into negotiations, I felt the Holy Spirit tell me not to ask Kenny for anything.

You read that right: not ask him for *anything*. Just earlier that day, I was praying with Earl, a friend of mine who is savvy with startup businesses. Several times before, in his own career, he had been in my position. As a result, he understood many of the nuances and much of the context of compensation conversations in a startup environment. He gave me some insight as to what was and was not reasonable to expect and ask for in this situation. In addition to my own research, I used his input to form the basis of my mental parameters for this upcoming conversation and possible negotiation with Kenny.

Additionally, Earl and I shared what I've found to be a very rare and similar "precious faith" (2 Peter 1:1). He had his own experiences and understanding of the seemingly insane decision-making that follows from a supernatural revelation of God's Grace. As is our tradition, we were wrapping up our conversation with prayer. In the middle of this prayer, I felt the Holy Spirit encourage me to trust Him completely to provide for my needs and wants without negotiating with Kenny. This required a much deeper level of trust and faith in God to receive whatever Kenny felt prompted to give me.

I knew how expensive that area of the country was, and based on all my research and many conversations with people, I also had a pretty definitive idea in my head of what was "fair and reasonable" compensation. So, leaving this completely up to somebody else's decision making did not appeal to my logical brain in the least. Yet, there was an undeniable peace that seemed to trump my human understanding, and I felt strongly that I was to follow that peace instead of my logical thinking. The apostle Paul wrote about this very thing in Philippians 4:6–7: "**Do not be anxious about anything**, but in every situation, by prayer and petition, with thanksgiving, present your requests to God. And the peace of God, which transcends all understanding, will guard your hearts and your minds in Christ Jesus" (NIV).

When I had the conversation over the phone with Kenny, knowing it made no sense but trusting God anyway, I began telling him what the Holy Spirit told me in prayer: not to ask him for anything but trust that whatever he offered me would be fair and more than enough to meet my needs. He was definitely taken aback and very grateful for my faith in God as well as my faith in him. He said he would think and pray about it over the next day or so and get back to me. A couple days turned into a couple more days, and pretty soon, it was over a week since we had talked.

I was really torn between just choosing to trust God completely and not worry about it because it wasn't going to affect my decision of whether or not to move from D.C. to Colorado. At the same time, I was on pins and needles waiting to hear what this man had decided.

I was heeding that call despite the doubt and discomfort that was trying to drown out the voice of faith within me.

I finally called him after about a week, "just to check in about our last conversation." He told me he had thought and prayed about it, and that he would be paying me $3,500 per month. That was quite a bit below my original "no less than" figure I had calculated, which very briefly gave me some concern. With my housing as cheap as it was, though, as well as the passive income I had from the VA, this would be more than enough to sustain me.

I should add that I was already a day or two from D.C. on my way to Colorado when I had that conversation, so it was similar to Cortez "burning the ships" when he got to the Americas. I was already past the point of no return, no matter the outcome of this conversation about my pay, on the road with everything I owned in my Honda Accord. I felt very much like Abraham, who left the land that was known and familiar to him for a very unknown future. But deep in my heart, I already knew that I was leaving D.C. and nothing was going to change that. So it really didn't matter what my employer did or didn't offer me; I had a call to head west, and I was heeding that call despite the doubt and discomfort that was trying to drown out the voice of faith within me.

When I got to Colorado, a few hours from my new home, I stopped to visit a friend named Riley I had known through a Bible study in the D.C. area. This would turn out to be a critical decision, though I couldn't have possibly known it at the time. All I knew was that Riley had left the D.C. area in 2014 so that he could go to a Bible college, despite the protests of many of his closest friends. Riley was in his 80s and knew the Word of God extremely well, so no one in our Bible study group could understand the draw for him to leave his entire life and move out to the other side of the country for something that seemed unnecessary. But he knew in his heart what God was telling him to do, and he wasn't going to let go of what God was leading him toward in the form of the desires within his heart (Psalms 37:4).

The thing that was remarkable to me about this encounter with my friend Riley at this Bible college was that I had been praying several years before about going to a Spirit-filled seminary. I was at a point where I had enough of intellectual, academic head knowledge and wanted four main things: the word of God, the Spirit of God, practical application, and a school that allowed me to use the GI Bill to pay for college and receive a housing allowance. I wanted nothing to do with the teachings of men, theologians, or abstract theory that added to my knowledge but did not edify my spirit. Incidentally, at the time, I was also looking at the idea of moving to Colorado.

Approximately two years later, here I am in Colorado visiting a friend at a Bible college. This Bible college eschewed the ineffective teachings of men and academic theory to focus exclusively on the Word of God, the Spirit of God, and practical application. And by the way, they had made certain provisions to allow veterans to use their VA benefits in the form of the GI Bill to have school paid for. This was exactly what I had been praying about several years before! I couldn't believe it.

And even more encouraging, not only my friend Riley but every other student that I saw on the campus that I visited was overflowing with life and energy about how amazing their experience was and how this Bible college had changed their lives. I felt an undeniable peace on that Colorado property in that small mountain town that I could not deny. As I was leaving to go to my new life in the Vail Valley, I'll never forget the way Riley looked me in the eye and said, "You'll be back." He said it with an utter confidence and finality that was not lost on me, and that I'll never forget. Be that as it may, I was due to report to my new job within the next week after I got settled in the generous accommodations God had provided for me. So it was with a bittersweet feeling in my heart that I said goodbye to Riley and this amazing school, which I had never before heard of, called Charis Bible College.

After less than a day's journey, I quickly got settled in to my new home in the town of Edwards, Colorado. The night I got there was memorable because there was a very rare blood moon. Many ministers and prophets had their own interpretations of what this meant, but to me, there was little doubt that it was significant from both a spiritual as well as an astronomical perspective. Genesis 1:14 says, "Then God said, 'Let there be light-bearers (sun, moon, stars) in the expanse of the heavens to separate the day from the night, and let them be useful for signs (tokens) [of God's provident care], and for marking seasons, days, and years'" (AMP). Though I didn't know the exact interpretation of what this rare lunar event signified, it certainly seemed symbolic and important as I was stepping into a new season of my life in so many ways on this exact day.

I quickly settled into my new home and started making connections at church and through business relationships in my role as sales and account manager for a new company in "the valley," as the Vail Valley in Eagle County, Colorado, was referred to. I was able to quickly establish a lot of personal and professional relationships in a pretty short amount of time, was doing really well in my job, and getting a lot of positive feedback from the owner and the partners of the business. I felt like I was "high on the mountaintop with God."

Yet, being in this new position started to bring out a lot of the old performance orientation and associated anxiety that constantly kept me on edge and made me my own worst taskmaster. I never felt like I was doing well enough or accomplishing enough, and it started to cause a lot of emotional and mental distress. Worst of all, I would take that with me into the workplace, and it would rub off on my immediate boss and caused him to feel like I was frustrated with him or other people.

It was bad enough that I was allowing performance to cause stress and negativity internally, but I was deeply convicted that my outward influence and witness to my boss (whom I greatly admired and really liked) was becoming toxic and negative. We were able to have a good conversation about it and realize we both were internalizing the same thing and that it was unnecessary, but I was back on that treadmill of performance anxiety and couldn't seem to shake it.

I started seeing a therapist about this, which still didn't seem to be able to get at the root of the issue. I wish I could have learned in the context of work performance to "be anxious for nothing," as the New King James Version words that same verse in Philippians 4:6. I can now see that my anxiety was truly "for *nothing*" since I was doing very well at my job and received frequent positive feedback. I think it's important to transparently share our struggles as well as our breakthroughs as we encourage others, which is why I share that with you as the reader. I definitely don't have it all figured out. However, one positive thing about this anxiety is that it drove me to seek God in daily, lengthy personal quiet times in the morning and cry out for His help.

In addition to anxiety, I was beginning to experience dissatisfaction and lack of fulfillment in my job and life in general. The ministry opportunity that had looked so promising had fallen through with little to no explanation. Despite all of the miraculous and exciting things that had unfolded recently, I was becoming acutely aware that if one is dissatisfied and discontent on the inside, nothing on the outside will ultimately change that. Moving to a beautiful area, having an amazing house to live in, doing an exciting and flexible job with

> *One positive thing about this anxiety is that it drove me to seek God.*

great coworkers, and participating in stimulating recreational activities can sometimes be a Band-Aid at best for a heart that is not fully alive and at peace. Circumstances, situations, outcomes (what I refer to as the "externals") somehow didn't seem to change what I was experiencing on the inside (what I refer to as the "inner life").

I was finding through direct personal experience and revelation that the old saying is so true: "Wherever you go, there you are." Though I wasn't necessarily benefiting from it, I was developing a greater appreciation and awareness for the fact that life has to be lived from the inside out, not the outside in. This was a painful but very good and necessary realization for me. I was coming to know without a doubt that if I were to continue staking my fulfillment and contentment on the externals, I would be chasing my tail for the rest of my life, constantly trying to eat the carrot that was always right in front of me but never totally within reach. Unfortunately, this wouldn't be the last time that I would become painfully aware of this truth, but it was the beginning of a life lesson I needed to learn.

After six months, it was time for me to find a new place to live, as my stay with my host family was intended to be transitional until I settled into the job and found a place of my own. A friend of mine became my roommate, and we found a fantastic apartment to live in. It was fully furnished, in a prime location right across from the gondola that goes up to Beaver Creek ski resort. It was a great deal, but significantly more expensive than my previous accommodations. Since I had been doing well in my job, Kenny and I had another conversation in which he agreed to raise my salary enough to cover the increase in my housing expenses.

My roommate and I moved in to our new apartment on April 1, 2016. Despite some of the anxiety and discouragement I had experienced during this season, it felt like things were falling into place and headed in a positive direction. My roommate and I got along well and really enjoyed our new place. He was also an avid skier, and we would regularly hit the slopes together. Due to an unusually high snowfall that year, Vail Ski Resort pushed back the closing day by an extra week, from April 7 to April 14. In fact, we got an amazing 11 inches of powder on Saturday, April 13. I was thrilled about this late season "epic dump" of powder, and my roommate and I join some others at Vail that day. Little did I know that before the end of that day, I would be wishing that Vail had closed as scheduled the week before...

PERSONAL REFLECTION AND PRACTICAL APPLICATION

If you struggle with anxiety in your work or personal life, lean into God on a daily basis. Even in the midst of high anxiety, God has been able to give me encouragement from His promise in Philippians 4:6–7, which says "<u>Be anxious for nothing</u>, but in everything by prayer and supplication, with thanksgiving, let your requests be made known to God; and the peace of God, which surpasses all understanding, will guard your hearts and minds through Christ Jesus." The process of overcoming anxiety may take time, but as you progress, it will be easier and easier to release your anxiety to God. Be patient with yourself in this process, as He is.

CHAPTER 13

DEEP IN THE VALLEY

The thing about an epic powder day is that everyone else wants to be on the mountain too. In a place as desirable and famous for skiing as Vail, this is especially true. To be able to get into those untapped powder stashes, you sometimes have to go off the beaten path between the trees. I would consider myself an intermediate-level snowboarder, so I still wasn't completely comfortable with my control of the board to perform the very quick turns necessary for that kind of maneuvering. But I was being intentional to continually learn and get better by pushing myself in going out with more experienced skiers and snowboarders on difficult runs and cutting between the trees.

On this particular day, I had been riding with my roommate and some other friends for a while and decided to break off by myself to take a run through the trees. I was enjoying the powder and becoming pretty confident in my turns, so I was feeling pretty good on the board. Unfortunately, I didn't see that in front of me was about a five-foot dropoff from the powder onto the packed snow on the groomed run. I landed hard on my left shoulder. It hurt pretty badly as soon as I landed, so I just laid there for a few moments to catch my breath and recover.

I unstrapped from the board to stand up and was able to raise both of my arms above my head. So far, so good. But within a minute or so, I noticed that my left shoulder was swelling up and tightening considerably. I was feeling more pain than usual from a normal, standard "wipeout." As I looked down, it seemed that my left arm was hanging lower than my right. About the same time, I started to feel queasy and clammy. I was pretty sure that my body was in the beginning phase of going into shock.

Luckily, I was close to a ski lodge. With the pain worsening moment by moment, I picked up my board and laboriously walked for what felt like an eternity the short distance to the lodge. My breathing was ragged and shallow, and it was an effort just to speak by the time I spoke to a ski patrol medic. Within a few moments of assessing me, he said that I had a noticeable "shelf" on my left shoulder and that it was almost certainly dislocated. I needed to get to the emergency room immediately. The ride down the mountain to get there was agonizing, as even the smallest bumps or movement caused excruciating pain.

After a painful ordeal waiting to be seen at the hospital, it turned out that a dislocated shoulder was actually the least of my problems. My humerus was fractured in three places and would need to be set in place with three metal screws. The doctor recommended surgery. After relocating my shoulder, they put me in a sling and sent me home with the pain at least manageable and the injury temporarily treated. I called my parents to tell them what happened, and my mom flew out to see me and help me through this. In typical male fashion, I thought she was overreacting and that it was unnecessary for her to do so. I would soon be extremely grateful that she had, though!

Once my mom got into town, we saw an orthopedic surgeon to have him evaluate the injury and get his recommendations. Part of the evaluation was a Magnetic Resonance Imaging (MRI) scan. The MRI revealed that, in addition to the bone fracture, my labrum had been torn. Of everything, this was by far the most serious and difficult aspect to the injury. The labrum is something akin to a ligament in the shoulder area. When my shoulder was dislocated, it had stretched out the labrum, which keeps the shoulder in place. We could set the bone in place with the insertion of metal screws, but there would always be a good chance my shoulder would pop out of place again if I didn't have surgery to tighten the labrum. I really wanted to avoid surgery, but when my mom asked the surgeon what he would recommend if it were his son, he said he would probably do the surgery. This surgeon is a world-renowned expert, and I got a really good feel from him, so I trusted his judgment. Based on that, we decided to go ahead and schedule the surgery.

Now the major challenge was being able to navigate the medical insurance to get a VA payment authorization for surgery, a very time-consuming and frustrating process that usually takes several weeks. After countless hours on the phone, hitting one roadblock after another, we finally found someone who was able to push the authorization through miraculously quickly. *Two days* later, I was in surgery. The surgeon said that he had never seen the VA move this quickly in his entire life and fully expected that we wouldn't be able to make it on the scheduled surgery date. This was undeniably God's grace and provision, for which my mom and I were extremely grateful.

The surgery took about three hours and went smoothly. I would need to be in a sling and have my shoulder completely immobilized for the next six weeks. The only exception was extremely painful physical therapy, which I had three times per week. Kenny graciously gave me a week off without charging me vacation time or docking my pay. I'd never had an injury or surgery of this magnitude before and didn't anticipate the mental and emotional toll it took in addition to the physical.

The most simple daily routines and actions are very difficult when you can't move one of your arms at all and incredibly painful when you have to (as is the case with showering). But I was extremely lucky and grateful to have the support of my mom for the time she was with me, as well as people from my church who dropped meals off for me on a daily basis for the next two weeks.

In addition to the psychological and physical effects this injury had on me, I was also very disappointed that I would not be able to enjoy all of the summer activities my friends were starting to get into after the ski season ended. People rightly say about the Vail Valley that you come for the winter, but you stay for the summer. I felt cooped up in the house and wished I could've been enjoying all of the fun new activities the summer brings to this amazing area. And it sounds weird to say it, but I felt emasculated in a way. Having this kind of injury somehow felt like it was robbing me of my masculinity and vitality. And the physical therapy regimen was more grueling and painful than I could've imagined. Slowly but surely, though, I recovered and gradually got back to work.

Before my injury, about the time I moved into my new apartment, we had been talking as a team about the need to pivot from our current business model and strategy. Expenses were two to three times what had been estimated, and revenues were far below projections. It was taking much longer than anticipated to get merchants onboarded to run offers through our mobile app and more expensive and time-consuming to acquire consumers that would purchase those offers. We realized that this model really needed to be introduced in a much larger market than the Vail Valley, so we began looking toward the "front range" of Denver and Colorado Springs to get a critical mass of merchants and consumers in creating this very challenging two-sided marketplace.

These kinds of business models (popularized by Groupon, Open Table, Airbnb, and other companies that generate their revenue by facilitating a transaction between two parties) are very high-risk, high reward. They can be extremely profitable when successfully executed on a large scale, but it's very difficult to get through the startup phase of building a wide enough user base to generate the high number of transactions required to financially support the business.

After about a week of being back at work full-time, Kevin told me we needed to schedule a conversation. When we sat down to talk, I could tell that he had a lot on his mind and sensed a heaviness over him. He told me had recently taken a vacation with his wife over a long weekend, during which he had been thinking and praying deeply about a lot of things. The cost overruns and underperformance of projected revenue had simply become unsustainable, especially since he was self-funding the majority of the startup's costs. We didn't have enough investors at this point to be able to continue operations with any reasonable hope of a major breakthrough anytime soon. As a result, he was shutting down the company in two weeks. He hoped that would be enough time for everybody to be able to get their affairs in order and find other jobs or sources of income.

I was taken completely off guard. I knew to an extent the business challenges we'd been facing, but didn't think it would come to this so quickly. I was also very concerned about the one-year lease I had just signed and how I was going to be able to pay for that. Despite my personal shock and disappointment, I felt a deep compassion for him. I could see how difficult it was for him to tell me this and how his eyes began to fill with tears when he did. I imagine he was battling a deep sense of discouragement and confusion after feeling like God had given him this idea he had invested so much blood, sweat, tears, and money into.

I tried to offer him some encouraging words and demonstrated my understanding. At the same time, I shared my concerns about having just signed an expensive lease based on the raise he had recently given me. He was very gracious and understanding and told me that he would be willing to pay all of my next month's housing costs to give me some breathing room in figuring out my situation. I expressed my sincere appreciation and gratitude for this, and we prayed briefly at the end of the conversation.

> *Everything that had looked like such a miraculous and promising new season of blessing and favor from God had just completely fallen apart.*

After I went home and contemplated all of this, I was completely at a loss. The ministry opportunity that had looked so promising had inexplicably fallen through, I was recovering from a traumatic injury, and now, I was out of a job. It seemed like everything that had looked like such a miraculous and promising new season of blessing and favor from God had just completely fallen apart. In less than nine months, I went from feeling like I was high on the mountaintop to being deep in the valley of despair. Next to the helicopter crash and my deployment to Afghanistan, this was one of the lowest points in my life. I knew—deep in my heart—that God had led me out here and orchestrated all of these open doors, but I could not make any sense of everything that had just happened. I fell into a darkness and depression born of confusion and discouragement.

King David of Israel wrote many psalms when he was in a place of deep darkness and despair within his soul. During these times, he poured out his heart to God with raw and vulnerable honesty, which helped him overcome his depression and discouragement. In Psalm 27:13–14 (NASB), he says, "I would have despaired unless I had believed that I would see the goodness of the Lord in the land of the living. Wait for the Lord; be strong and let your heart take courage; yes, wait for the Lord." Talking to God honestly from my heart and waiting on Him is what I attempted to do in the middle of this discouragement. I also saw a Christian counselor, which put things into perspective and took some of the sting out of my heart.

And like David, I saw "the goodness of the Lord in the land of the living." God had an ace up His sleeve that I didn't yet know about.

PERSONAL REFLECTION AND PRACTICAL APPLICATION

Do you feel like the bottom has just dropped out from underneath you, as though everything in your life seems to be falling apart? Are you in a valley of deep darkness and despair? Don't feel guilty or condemned by it, but pour out your heart openly and honestly to the Lord about it. Like David does so many times in the psalms, this can be powerfully therapeutic and help anchor your soul to the hope

"I would have despaired unless I had believed that I would see the goodness of the Lord in the land of the living. Wait for the Lord; be strong and let your heart take courage; yes, wait for the Lord."

you have in Jesus. You may also benefit from seeing a therapist, counselor, or friends and family you trust who can offer you much-needed encouragement and perspective. Believe that, like David in Psalm 27:13–14, you <u>will</u> see "the goodness of the Lord in the land of the living. Wait for the Lord; be strong and let your heart take courage; yes, wait for the Lord."

CHAPTER 14

THROUGH THE VALLEY

In the midst of this dark time for my troubled soul, I was once again driven to seek God in prayer, reading the Word, journaling, and meditating on His promises and what the Holy Spirit was speaking to my heart. Initially, I updated my resume and applied to several jobs. But as I spent increasing amounts of time in my recently wide-open schedule with the Lord, I felt the Holy Spirit prompt me to stop trying to do what I felt was the "responsible thing" and continue to spend time with Him. I'm the kind of person who needs a lot of structure in my daily activity or else I can fall into a state of complacency and stagnancy when I don't have an external requirement to show up somewhere at a set time for a specific reason.

If I never left the house all day and did nothing but spend time with Him, that would be the most productive thing I could possibly do.

So even though it was difficult for me to sit inside, especially when it was so beautiful outside in such a beautiful area, I felt the Lord telling me that if I never left the house all day and did nothing but spend time with Him, that would be the most productive thing I could possibly do. As I reluctantly submitted to this process, I felt a renewed stirring to find some kind of program or school that would sharpen my skill sets in a practical way, in an environment with other people that were pursuing their dreams leading to personal relationships that could open doors of opportunity. I started to do some research online about various programs, but even then, I felt the Holy Spirit's prompting not to try to figure it out on my own, but that He would "drop something in my lap" that would be much better than anything I could come up with in my own human abilities.

Once again, even though I felt like I was hearing from God, it ran totally counter to all of my human thinking and inclinations to be responsible and get something done in a practical sense. It was very reminiscent of my time at the monastery only a year before this, and I couldn't believe that I could doubt so much after seeing God do such amazing things the last time. I was really struggling with it, so I decided to reconnect with my friend Earl in D.C. whose perspective helped me when I was considering my possible negotiation with Kenny about my compensation. I felt like it was important for me to get some outside perspective and counsel from someone who could tell me if there were any blind spots in my thinking. I'm a big believer in the wisdom of the verse that says, "Where no wise guidance is, the people falleth; but in the multitude of counsellors there is safety" (Proverbs 11:14 ASV).

I told Earl about everything that had happened and my struggle to "wait around for God" to once again drop something in my lap. He encouraged me that if I was spending time with God and trusted what He was telling me, then that's what I needed to do. We had a really great conversation for about an hour and a half. Just as we were getting off the phone, he made an offhand comment about somebody who he was potentially going to interview for his radio show. This interviewee was a career military veteran who had gone through a program in Georgetown, D.C., for transitioning military veterans looking for next steps in their life, with an emphasis on business and entrepreneurship. The organization is called Dog Tag, Inc., and the program is the Dog Tag Fellowship Program.

It actually sounded like a program that could be very beneficial and one for which I could be a qualified candidate. I asked him if he thought I would be eligible for it, and he stopped for a moment. He said, "Oh my gosh, I think we were supposed to have this conversation." He told me he would send an email to the CEO of the program and ask about it. Within a few minutes, I received an email from the CEO of the program saying that she thought I would be an excellent candidate and that we should talk very soon. We had a phone call within the next day or two, and she told me more about the program. I had gone on the website and looked at information about it and was wondering if I really qualified. She assured me that I did and said that there was a spot open for the January fellowship. This would give me about six months to get everything in order and be ready to head out. The CEO told me she wanted to schedule another phone call with the program director and me to talk further about it.

A day or two later, I spoke with the program director, and she confirmed very strongly she thought I would be a perfect fit. She also told me that they had a last-second opening for the next cohort, which started about 10 days later. My immediate thought was that there was no way I could possibly make that opportunity happen, but she urged me to just think about it and let her know if my position about it changed. Just like in the instance of going to South America to see my sister on vacation, I left the door just barely cracked for the Holy Spirit to set everything in order and give me the peace and confirmation to move forward if that was His will. I spoke with my parents about it, and they were excited and thought it would be a good thing if all the details could be worked out.

There was only one snag: I was already booked on a flight to go to the beach in Oregon with my extended family that would take me out of the fellowship program for a week right after it had started. I prayed with my family and decided if there was any way I could still be able to take that vacation while working out the details of the move, I would seriously consider it. After speaking with the program director about it, she said that although it wasn't ideal

> *I told Him that the pressure and responsibility was on Him and that I would not take on that responsibility.*

to take so much time off so early in the program, they did allow fellows to take a week of personal time at some point during the fellowship and that we could make it work. I told her I still had a lot of details to work out, but if I could make everything align, I would seriously consider it.

I still had several seemingly insurmountable barriers to overcome. First off, I needed to find somebody to replace me on my one-year lease. I knew it needed to be somebody that my existing roommate would know and get along with well. Secondly, I needed to find affordable housing that was close to the fellowship in D.C. on extremely short notice. This by itself seemed impossible. Lastly, I had no idea how I would be able to pack all of my stuff up with my shoulder injury still a major factor.

So, I told God that I was open to do this if *He* would put everything in order, and I didn't have to bend over backwards and stress out about it. I told Him that the pressure and responsibility was on *Him* and that I would not take on that responsibility. But I resolved in my heart that I would be a willing and available vessel if He could line it all up. I made a deal with God that if we could get the housing situation settled in Colorado and I could somehow get all packed up with my injured shoulder, I would trust Him enough to make the move even if I didn't yet have a place identified to live in D.C.

During this same timeframe, one of my good friends Dave mentioned that he was thinking about moving out of his existing place. I told him about this potential opportunity, and he loved my place, but didn't think he'd have enough money to pay the deposit or my portion of the rent. I asked my existing roommate, Kam, if he would be okay with having Dave as a roommate, and he was thrilled with the possibility. He was also willing to pay a little bit more in rent to offset Dave's portion of it. The landlord was also very amenable to the proposal. I told Dave that I would cover his deposit, and Kam would be willing to pay a little bit more on his end for rent. Kam and Dave helped me pack up my things and get them in the car. Even without their help at times, I was pleasantly surprised by how much I could get done by myself, even with my shoulder injury. 2 Chronicles 16:9 (DRC 1752) says, "For the eyes of the Lord behold all the earth, and give strength to those who with a perfect heart trust in him..." Within just a few days, God had worked everything out!

Through God's grace and a place of personal humility, once again, my investment in rest paid huge dividends.

It was a win for everybody involved. I literally could not have scripted a more perfect roommate for Kam or overall situation if I tried, so I knew God was being faithful to take care of me and everyone else involved. With all that settled, I enthusiastically told the program director and CEO I would be happy to be a part of Dog Tag, Inc.'s Cohort 4. About a week after my initial conversation with Earl, I was all packed up and headed back across the country for the next phase of the journey. Through God's grace and a place of personal humility, once again, my investment in rest paid huge dividends.

Sometimes, life seems to come in very fast and intense seasons. In a very short time, I had gone from being high on the mountaintop to deep in the valley and was now moving through the valley to a place of new promise. In many ways, this season was very similar to the season of resting and trusting God after I got back from the monastery. In both cases, the process involved a high degree of uncertainty and major life change. In both cases, this walk of faith led me across the country between D.C. and Colorado. The difference was that last time, the whole process took about five months. This time, it all happened in about three weeks!

I've personally found that my faith muscles are increasingly built from rest instead of exertion.

Similar to how our physical bodies develop in the natural realm, the more we exercise our faith muscles, the stronger and more responsive they become to trusting God at greater levels in shorter time frames. Unlike the natural realm, I've personally found that my faith muscles are increasingly built from rest instead of exertion. This has increasingly become a counterintuitive but critical aspect of my spiritual growth and maturity, helping me perceive reality according to God's perspective instead of my own.

Hebrews 5:14 (TPT) says, "For every spiritual infant who lives on milk is not yet pierced by the revelation of righteousness. But solid food is for the mature, **whose spiritual senses perceive heavenly matters.** And they have been **adequately trained by what they've experienced** to emerge with understanding of the difference between what is truly excellent and what is evil and harmful" (my emphasis). The more you receive a revelation of grace and your righteousness in Christ, the more you can trust the inner witness of the Holy Spirit in your spiritual senses despite your natural senses and human thinking patterns.

Whether it's a short and intense season like this was for me or a longer period of struggle like I experienced in Afghanistan or the Pentagon, I want you to know that despite your circumstances in the natural, **there is hope**. Be encouraged that if you are going through it right now, the good news

If you're deep in the valley of darkness and despair, God's grace and constant presence will get you through that valley eventually.

is… you're going *through* it. You can have the same confidence in God as David did when he said, "Even though I walk through the darkest valley, I will fear no evil, for you are with me; your rod and your staff, they comfort me" (Psalm 23:4).

If you're deep in the valley of darkness and despair, God's grace and constant presence will get you through that valley eventually. The more you walk by faith in letting go and resting in God's amazing grace, the more He can set you up for journeys you never would have unanticipated, with far better outcomes than anything you could have imagined. Never stop trusting and resting in God, and the "rest" will take care of itself.

PERSONAL REFLECTION AND PRACTICAL APPLICATION

If you're deep in the valley of darkness and despair, meditate on David's words in Psalm 23:4: "Even though I walk through the darkest valley, I will fear no evil, for you are with me; your rod and your staff, they comfort me." With the same intentionality and focus you would use your natural muscles through physical training of your body to overcome resistance, focus on using your "spiritual senses to perceive heavenly matters, being adequately trained by what you've experienced" (Hebrews 5:14). Many times "dark valleys" can provide the greatest spiritual "resistance training." In the spiritual realm, though, faith muscles are sometimes most powerfully developed through rest instead of exertion. My personal testimony and encouragement is that you will make it through the valley. Rest in God's presence, and let the "rest" take care of itself!

CHAPTER 15

MY PLACE CALLED "THERE"

Less than a year after leaving the D.C. area for Colorado, I was now on my way from Colorado *back* to D.C. I still hadn't found a place to live there, but my "deal" with God was that, if He would work things out in getting someone to replace me on my existing lease, I would trust Him to provide a new place back in the D.C. area. It was a step of faith, for sure, but not as difficult now that I had seen Him work everything else out to this point.

I was staying the night at a motel in Pennsylvania the night before getting to D.C. My close friend in D.C. texted to ask me where I was, how things were going, and if I had found a place to live yet. I told him I was about eight hours from D.C. and was still trusting God to provide a place to live. He called me right then to tell me he had just moved into a nice apartment and that I was welcome to stay with him until I could find my own place. He also said that he was about to go on vacation for several weeks and that I'd have the place to myself during that time! In a way, I couldn't believe it, but I also knew by now that I should fully expect God to provide for me the practical things He knows I need as I focused on seeking Him and following His guidance and direction for my life.

In Matthew 6:33 (TPT), Jesus says, "So above all, constantly chase after the realm of God's kingdom and the righteousness that proceeds from him. Then all these less important things will be given to you abundantly." A place to live seemed to me a very important thing, but in God's Kingdom, it's considered a "less important thing" that will be provided simply as the outflow or byproduct of seeking Him above all else. Through this experience, He was showing me His faithfulness and provision in making good on that promise.

The other huge benefit to me of this was that this particular friend of mine shared a deep and abiding revelation of staying in God's grace and rest, so it was very edifying for both of us to have long conversations about all this as we processed these deep truths of the "too good to be true news" of the Gospel. Plus, I had built-in fellowship for a new season of life in a familiar but nonetheless new area. And of course, I was blessed with the financial benefit of having a nice place to stay in a very expensive area, rent-free for a time.

Within a few days, I started the Fellowship Program at Dog Tag Inc. in Georgetown. This was the program I had been led to pray and believe for back in Colorado when I was in the midst of navigating my transition. This program was specifically for military veterans, their spouses and/or caregivers, and defense linguists (translators from other countries who contracted with the Defense Department). It was designed as a holistic program to assist us in transitioning from military service to a post-military life, with an emphasis on business and entrepreneurship. The fellowship is funded through a non-profit entity called Dog Tag Inc. that gives fellows a stipend for living expenses and provided a totally free program.

This program consists of three main components. The first is a Certificate of Business Administration through Georgetown's School of Continuing Studies, through which Georgetown business professors come to the bakery where we attended class to teach different business courses. The second is through the for-profit entity Dog Tag Bakery, whereby we participated in an experiential learning program by learning about and being involved with the real-world bakery so we can learn different aspects of small business ownership and management. The third component is learning labs where outside instructors come in to share their business, work, and life experiences to help us be prepared and equipped for success after the fellowship. There's also a wellness component to the program that helps us make sense of our life stories and experiences as we chart a new course in living a purposeful and productive life.

> *A plan (motive, wise counsel) in the heart of a man is like water in a deep well, but a man of understanding draws it out.*

Through this fellowship program, I was exposed to other outside organizational partners, with the option to participate in extracurricular activities to enhance and supplement the learning process through the fellowship. One of these outside organizations is Capital Post, which hosted a coaching program called "RESET." Through RESET, I was able to work with a personal and professional coach who helped me gain more self-awareness through different tools and engagements to hone in more on my personal values and vision. In conjunction with personal coaching sessions with the Dog Tag Program Director, I was able to gain additional clarity and articulate what I wanted to do for my life's work.

As an aspiring coach myself, this was a valuable learning experience not only as a client but also as a future coach. Proverbs 20:5 (AMP) says, "A plan (motive, wise counsel) in the heart of a man is like water in a deep well, but a man of understanding draws it out." This is what a good coach should be able to do: through penetrating questions and insightful feedback, draw out of the clients what is deep within them to gain a different and helpful perspective of themselves and how to proceed. The RESET coach also helped me craft a speech for my Georgetown Business Communications class. This assignment was to give a three-to-five minute persuasive speech in a business context, incorporating the class material. I greatly benefitted from her insight and questions in coming up with a personally meaningful and relevant topic for my speech.

Prayer should be the number one priority for every Christian business owner.

As a result, I wrote my persuasive speech on "why prayer should be the number one priority for every Christian business owner." Based on my recent revelations in this season of life, my goal was to show that prayer can have extremely practical and measurable bottom-line results and outcomes. As research for this assignment, I found a ministry website that had astounding testimonies and case studies of just that. I was amazed by the clear connection between the prayers of the ministry leaders and their business clients with very specific business metrics and testimonies of how prayer and faith had miraculously prospered these businesses. I had hit solid gold! The combination of personal coaching, the academic assignment, and these testimonies I learned of through that process were life-changing. Though I didn't know it at the time, this would serve as the seeds of what eventually became *A Better Way.*

Until this time, I had been fighting a desire to go to a Bible college or an immersive spiritual program like Bethel Church's School of Supernatural Ministry, Youth With A Mission, or the International House of Prayer's internship and worship schools. I called these types of programs and environments "Christian bubbles." Though I really had a desire in my heart for something like this, I had seen many people go through these different programs and have an amazing experience during their time but didn't seem to do much with it that transformed their lives in a practical and sustainable way afterward. It seemed to me like it was really easy to be a Christian in the "bubble," but it didn't have the outcomes for a lot of people I desired for myself.

Another issue I was working through at Dog Tag as I developed my message and target audience was that I didn't want to just be "preaching to the choir" of an all-Christian audience. At the same time, I knew that my relationship with Jesus and my faith based on scriptural truths were core to my message and content. I didn't know how to stay true to my beliefs and convictions in a way that would not alienate non-Christians.

At this time, my fellowship cohort was nearing the end of the five-month fellowship. I was constantly thinking ahead to what I would do once I graduated and specifically how I could make that pay the bills in a very expensive city. I began to deal with a lot of anxiety over this as I tried to force things to work out on a specific timeline, not knowing what was next or how it would all work out. The stress, confusion, and uncertainty was once again starting to overwhelm me.

In discussing all this during my personal coaching sessions with the program director at Dog Tag, a transformative realization emerged, which was to "embrace the bubble." My coach encouraged me that I didn't have to have all this figured out from day one. She used the example of John Maxwell, a Christian pastor who has gone on to become one of the world's foremost experts on leadership development. She encouraged me that, like Maxwell, I could start with a very specific target audience and message. Through that process, I could trust that eventually I would reach a much larger audience with a powerful message that would be personally and professionally relevant and beneficial to them.

I needn't worry about trying to "get out there" and reach everyone immediately, but I could actually benefit from a time of being in a "bubble" environment. The bubble could act as a greenhouse to cultivate my vision and lead to strategic relationships in an environment of like-minded people that would lead to greater opportunities to eventually go well beyond the bubble. This freed me up to discard a well-intentioned but misguided belief that I needed to "fight the bubble" and get right into the nitty gritty world of business by trying to make an immediate impact by being all things to all people. I finally was able to give myself permission to stop working against the grain of my natural inclinations and heart's deep desires. This was so liberating and life-giving for me!

> *I finally was able to give myself permission to stop working against the grain of my natural inclinations and heart's deep desires.*

At the same time, I got back in touch with a friend named Frank who had moved from D.C. to Colorado to attend Charis Bible College. I had told Frank about Charis earlier when I visited my friend Riley on the way to Vail and let him know that he could use his GI Bill to pay for school. Ironically, right after I got back to D.C. from Vail, he was just about to leave D.C. for Colorado to attend Charis. As I was finishing up at Dog Tag, we caught up over the phone, and Frank was telling me about his first term at Charis. Talking to him about it reminded me of the deep sense of confirmation and peace I had felt when I was visiting Riley about a year prior. Frank told me that students who hadn't been able to make it in time for the start of the fall term in September could start at the beginning of the winter term at the end of November.

All of a sudden, it hit me like a ton of bricks: Why not just apply to Charis? I already knew that was a place that seemed to be "calling" to me, and I was experiencing nothing but frustration and anxiety thinking about what I would do in D.C.

after I graduated Dog Tag. It was only a month prior to the start of the winter term, and I didn't know if that would give me enough time to apply, be accepted to the college, and also have the VA process the necessary paperwork for me to be able to use the GI Bill. But I had seen God move miraculously fast in my move from Vail to D.C. for Dog Tag, so I thought "why not at least try and see what happens?"

My thought was that if I were somehow to get everything in order to attend Charis and no other compelling opportunities were presented to me in D.C., I would consider that a strong indication that this would be a good path. Again, I adopted the mentality that I didn't know if this was possible, but I would just "cast my bread on the waters" and see what returned. Like my last move, I was just keeping an open hand and trusting that if this was from God, His grace would set everything in place to facilitate it, no matter the obstacles or the timeline.

Two weeks later, I had been accepted to Charis and was assured that the GI Bill paperwork would go through in time to have all my school expenses paid for, as well as a housing allowance to supplement income. Between the VA benefits I already had and the housing allowance, I would have more than enough to allow me to go to school full-time. Not only that, I had some family friends in Colorado Springs (about 30 minutes from Charis) who said I could live in their house until I found my own place. This took a lot of the pressure off me with the short timeline in getting out there (does that sound familiar?). Once again, God took my mustard seed of faith and used it to open doors for me to walk the path He had for me.

Andrew Wommack has a teaching about 1 Kings 17, in which the Old Testament prophet Elijah supernaturally spoke forth a drought in the land. The Word of the Lord then came to Elijah and specifically directed him to another land, where he was to be supernaturally nourished with food and water: "You will drink from the brook, and I have directed the ravens to supply you with food *there*" (1 Kings 17:4, my emphasis). As Wommack teaches, you may receive a word from the Lord to move from where you are to a specific place, at a specific time, for a specific reason. Whether

If the place where you currently are is "drying up," it may be a sign that it's time for you to move on to a new place.

it's literally/geographically or metaphorically, if the place where you currently are is "drying up," it may be a sign that it's time for you to move on to a new place where God's supernatural provision is waiting for you, for a specific purpose. Like Elijah, God's grace for you is "there."

I can relate to that in a fairly dramatic way. God's grace mysteriously but clearly lifted off my real estate practice in the D.C. area and led me to Colorado for the startup job. On my way "there," I was divinely intersected with Charis Bible College. Though God didn't cause my injury or the failure of the business I was working for in Vail, there was an undeniable sense of timing and grace leading me back to D.C. for a specific purpose at that specific time. Finally, it became painfully obvious at a certain time that D.C. was becoming a "dry" place for me, and once again, there was peace and confirmation about moving back to Colorado a second time. In retrospect, I now see so clearly how God had a specific and divine purpose in leading me to each of those places at the time and in the order which He did.

I got to Colorado Springs right before the winter school term started in late November 2016. It felt right being back in Colorado—like being home. As it says on the front gate coming into Charis Bible College, I was in my place called "there."

Personal Reflection and Practical Application

Are you in a place that's feeling spiritually or otherwise "dry"? Ask God if it's because your place called "there" has moved somewhere else. If so, God will speak to you just as He spoke to Elijah about when and where to go (1 Kings 17:4). The presence or absence of His peace, joy, and desire in your heart will make it abundantly clear at just the right time where He's taking you away from as well as where He's leading you toward. Where God guides, He provides; if it's really God's grace, you won't need to force anything to make it happen. He will open doors for you so effortlessly you won't be able to miss it. If *you're* the one *forcing* doors open or shut, pray about whether it's really God leading you to move somewhere else. He's perfectly willing and able to make Himself known to you, primarily through the inner witness of the Holy Spirit and also through external factors. No matter how crazy or illogical it may seem, His perfect peace will guide you into all truth and intersect you with the dreams and desires He Himself put within you for a specific purpose.

CHAPTER 16

THE SEED WITHIN

It was surreal and refreshing to be back in Colorado, the place I had fallen in love with when I was in the Vail Valley. What a whirlwind journey and adventure the Lord had taken me on: first from the D.C. area to Colorado, then from Colorado to D.C., and finally from D.C. *back* to Colorado, all in 14 months! Some of my friends couldn't keep up with me anymore with all my address changes and moves across the country. I even felt somewhat foolish bouncing around like a pinball from one place to another so suddenly and frequently.

"O LORD, I know the way of man is not in himself; it is not in man who walks to direct his own steps."

I suspect that some people who know me may have questioned my stability or wisdom during this time, and I wouldn't blame them if they did. But time and again, I have seen that amazing things happen when we walk increasingly by faith and not sight, laying aside our own human thinking and deferring to the Holy Spirit's leading. Jeremiah 10:23 says, "O LORD, I know the way of man is not in himself; it is not in man who walks to direct his own steps." To say the least!

If I had been "walking to direct my own steps," it would have made so much more sense to go three hours in a straight line from the Vail Valley to Charis in Woodland Park. But God does not always work in a linear fashion. In the moment, it can seem like He's taking us backwards or on a detour, but later, we can see a bigger picture and a pattern we couldn't recognize at the time. Sometimes, I think God has to take us out of where we are and place us somewhere else just to turn around and put us right back where we originally were.

The difference isn't so much in where we are or what we're doing but in *who* we're *becoming* through that process. I later recognized that I needed to go through an inner journey of changing my thinking ("repenting") so that I was where I needed to be on the *inside* (my heart attitude and mental paradigm) when I got to where I was going on the *outside* (whatever external circumstance and/or geographical location I ended up in). My perspective needed to shift in addition to my circumstances: the personal interactions and growth process that I experienced in DC while going through Dog Tag prepared me to transition into the next step of attending Charis. Thanks to the process, when I got back to Colorado I was at a place of peace, joy, and "settledness" in my heart and mind, and able to fully embrace the coming season.

On a practical level, I had some critical learning experiences in D.C. that resulted in profound revelations I probably would not otherwise have had. The revelation—in this case, catalyzed by the Georgetown Communications class assignment and research for that speech—was in seed form in that season. By putting myself in a "greenhouse" environment in the next chapter of my life at Charis (a

The difference isn't so much in where we are or what we're doing but in who we're becoming through that process.

situation that I previously would have derisively referred to as a "bubble"), that seed was able to be nurtured and grow at an accelerated rate. Being saturated in God's Word through Bible college classes for four hours every weekday in a spiritually charged atmosphere with people from all over the world who had made a similar pilgrimage watered that seed and gave it rich nutrients to sprout and flourish.

Case in point: Fairly soon after arriving at Charis, as I was praying and journaling, the Lord brought to my mind the revelation I received while working on the Georgetown University Communications class assignment. I felt a prompting to ask on a Charis community Facebook page for testimonies anyone had in which prayer had made a miraculous and practical impact in their business. This idea was in such embryonic form that, at first, I hesitated: I thought I needed something more substantive and specific before I posted about it publicly. I wanted something more well-defined or developed before I was comfortable moving forward.

I felt a strong conviction not to overthink it (something I tend to do quite a bit) and just take tiny, simple steps of obedience with what I had. The Lord humored me enough to help me quickly draft a half-page document giving some really basic parameters for what I was seeking. I posted it on the Facebook page and eventually received a few responses from people in my Bible college class. Even then, I didn't really know what I was supposed to *do* with it. So, I just wrote down a paragraph or so covering the highlights of different testimonials, similar to client testimonials you might see on a business website.

But again, it wasn't so important what I was "doing" externally during that time as it was the "inner life" I was cultivating by intentionally thinking about and meditating on the revelation. And as I did so, naturally I couldn't help but talk about it. And the more I talked about it with people, the more they either shared their own stories or referred me to other people they knew who had testimonies that fit the criteria I felt the Lord had given me.

After writing down a handful of testimonies from different people and compiling them into a Word document, I met a guy named Rodney who had an amazing story but wasn't as communicative through writing or the written word. However, he was extremely personable and engaging face to face, so I booked a conference room at a public library and just used my phone to record a video of him telling his story.

The interview ended up being about 30 minutes long and perfectly captured the essence of this budding message God had put in my heart. (You can listen to this inspiring and remarkable story from Rodney Ranney on the podcast: ABW 11 – God Uses the Simple to Confound the Wise). It was a perfect medium for Rodney because of his personality. But even more than that, I cannot even describe to you the high I was experiencing from doing the interview. It was intoxicating! I knew that Rodney wasn't the only one in his element, and it was starting to feel like I was really on to something, working in my gifting and calling but in a way like never before.

After that, I did another interview with an incredible salesman and integrous man of God named Jim who had one remarkable testimony after another. This time, I recorded just the audio on my phone since we were at school in a busy and noisy area. We talked and recorded about 90 straight minutes of inspiring and miraculous testimonies about his business where the supernatural met the practical and people were blessed beyond belief in all kinds of ways. I noticed that, as we did this, that high was back, and I could tell that *he* felt it too! I even remarked to Jim right after we finished the interview that I could almost see myself being a radio show host or something.

He agreed but then proceeded to throw out this little question: "Or what about a podcast?" Hmmm… what about it, indeed! This was, after all, 2017. That seemed more relevant and achievable. The only thing was, I had barely ever *listened* to any podcasts at that time, let alone created and hosted one. I had absolutely no idea how any of that worked. But I couldn't deny the passion, excitement, and energy that was bubbling out of me from having these engaging conversations with people about this topic I loved. And more than

_____

***God** was at the center of it all, being glorified through His almost too-crazy-to-believe goodness.*

_____

that, it was evident that as I engaged the interviewees in these conversations, *they* were coming alive before my eyes. And most importantly, **God** was at the center of it all, being glorified through His almost *too*-crazy-to-believe goodness.

But what happened next was over-the-top. I had been talking to a classmate of mine who had an astounding story of how he created a million-dollar business that he started at the age of 16. He was in a financial bind at the time and needed to make some money to pay some bills. So, with no experience whatsoever, he just decided that websites seemed to be a good way to make money and just walked in off the street to pitch this idea to a business owner. Somehow, the guy gave him several thousand dollars to create a website, and he was off to the races.

Within three years, he had an extremely profitable business with over one hundred clients. He was charging tens of thousands of dollars for a single website. But his heart was to help people and sow into their God-given vision, so he blessed many people by doing it for free or charging extremely low fees. This just came back around and blessed him with more clients, more revenue for his business, and more opportunities to speak and minister at a very young age in an internationally renowned megachurch.

But that's not all. As I interviewed him on my humble little iPhone for 10 minutes or so about this mind-blowing story, he also "caught the bug" of that energy and passion I had experienced with previous interviewees. In fact, after the interview, he was so inspired by the vision of what God had put in my heart to share with people that he wanted to sow into my "ministry" (as he called it, even though I hadn't thought of it in that way until right then). He offered right there on the spot to build me a beautiful and functional website for *free*. Not only that, but he had helped hundreds of previous clients launch podcasts, books, online courses, and teaching materials, and he offered to do that for me as well!

That's when things got real for me. Just a month or two previously, I had started all this by simply writing down a few sentences to capture the highlights of people's stories. Then I just recorded audio or video on my phone, still not having any idea what to do with it. Now I was being offered the chance to have a full-blown website and podcast launched from scratch (that I had no idea how to create on my own) by a very successful entrepreneur and web designer extraordinaire who had charged many people tens of thousands of dollars for the same services. He even had an expensive studio-quality microphone he would let me use whenever I wanted. And did I mention that he was going to do it all for *free*?!

What had been on the inside of me in seed form was now manifesting externally in a very real and powerful way. By that summer, I had not only a podcast but also a professional website with a secure online payment portal, an LLC, business cards, and my first business checking account all set up and ready to go. To my astonishment, I was now officially and legally a business owner and podcast host! Never in a million years (or even six months prior) would I have believed anyone who told me that I would be creating and hosting a podcast or have my own website, company, or "ministry." But as I mentioned at the beginning of this chapter, miraculous things happen when you let go of your human thinking and follow the inner witness of peace, joy, and desire the Holy Spirit plants within your heart. What if I had never stepped out like the Holy Spirit had prompted me? What if I had believed the lie that everything needed to "make sense" or "be better organized" before I could act on the idea that God gave me?

He will lead you on a bread crumb trail of adventure into unfamiliar territory that you never would have thought to follow on your own. By taking small, simple steps of obedience without knowing where it's all going, He will supernaturally open up doors of opportunity and effortlessly intersect you with the right people and situations that will bring what's inside your heart in seed form to practical manifestation. And even though it happens in a way you never would have expected, it somehow also bears witness with a deep inner knowing that this is exactly the path you should be on.

> *Miraculous things happen when you let go of your human thinking and follow the inner witness of peace, joy, and desire the Holy Spirit plants within your heart.*

As I listened to the still, small voice of God's Spirit and walked this unlikely step-by-step path with Him, He revealed to me desires, gifts, and vision I didn't even know I had inside me. Jesus speaks about this:

> He said, 'How will we liken the Kingdom of God? Or with what parable will we illustrate it? It's like a grain of mustard seed, which, when it is sown in the earth, though it is less than all the seeds that are on the earth, yet when it is sown,

grows up, and becomes greater than all the herbs, and puts out great branches, so that the birds of the sky can lodge under its shadow'" (**Mark 4:30–32, World English Bible**).

In this scripture as well as other passages in the Bible, a seed is used as an illustration of the Word of God and our faith. That was certainly true for me in this process I've just described. But I've heard it said that a seed can be many things: money, time, attitude, focus, or even a smile. In this case, I also think that God-given revelation, passions, gifts, talents, personality traits, and godly relationships were also seeds.

> *The outcomes that represent God's best for us are not only something we don't have to earn or work hard for; they're things we can't even earn or work hard for.*

It required the illumination of God's Truth through the Holy Spirit and His Word in the context of many unexpected and unfamiliar experiences to create a newfound awareness of that seed within me. Though it usually starts out small and grows ever so slowly, it can suddenly manifest all at once if we keep watering and nurturing it.

The wondrous nature of all this to me is that there was no striving, toiling, or even "trying" on my part to manifest any of this. At least, it didn't feel like that to me. And that's the amazing thing about God's grace: The outcomes that represent God's best for us are not only something we don't *have* to earn or work hard for; they're things we *can't* even earn or work hard for. God's grace, by its very definition, is something that is nullified and impossible to receive as a result of our own human effort and toil.

To continue with the agricultural analogies, fruit doesn't— and *can't*—grow by being forced to. The branches on grape vines aren't straining to produce or grow the grapes. It is entirely a natural process that is simply the result of the branch being connected to the vine. When the branch is connected—or *one*—with the vine, the inevitable and effortless result is that it will bear fruit. The nutrients from the vine are transmitted to, and then through, the branches. The only thing that can prevent a branch from bearing fruit is being cut off from the vine.

Jesus says, "Remain in me, as I also remain in you. No branch can bear fruit by itself; it must remain in the vine. Neither can you bear fruit unless you remain in me. I am the vine; you are the branches. If you remain in me and I in you, you will bear much fruit; apart from me you can do nothing. If you do not remain in me, you are like a branch that is thrown away and withers; such branches are picked up, thrown into the fire and burned" (John 15:4–5). The metaphors Jesus uses are so transferable in describing deeper and more substantive spiritual truths that it's almost like God invented these natural laws and organic processes just to give us an illustration of our relationship with Him.

Whether or not that's true, the point remains that living a Spirit-filled and Spirit-led life of fruitfulness and godliness is inherently *designed* to be as natural and effortless for us as bearing fruit is for a branch connected to a vine or tree. Contrary to the lies perpetrated upon us by the spirit of religion, man-made traditions, and our "flesh" (human tendencies when *disconnected* from God), this is the Truth: ***It's not <u>supposed</u> to be hard to live our lives in God!*** If we, as branches, are simply connected to and living from the "nutrients" Jesus gives us as the True Vine, it's impossible *not* to be fruitful.

When we are in union or oneness with Him, it's almost like we become a divine-human hybrid organism. It's hard to tell where He stops and we begin. His desires become our desires, and therefore, those desires are fulfilled by Him: in, for, and through us unto the blessing and edification of others (after all, the fruit isn't for the vine or the branch that produced it). We have become part of and one with the Body of Christ, which strengthens and builds itself up as the various parts working together as one living organism. This is true at the individual level as well as the corporate level.

This is why I so emphatically emphasize God's grace and rest in this book, the blog, and the podcast. Hopefully, I've given more context from scripture as well as the personal experiences from my own life and other people's lives about that seemingly heretical statement I made at the very beginning of Chapter 1: *Hard work is ungodly.* Not because God wants us to be passive, unproductive, or inconsequential, but because the life energy that flows through the Vine to the branches that facilitates the fruit-bearing process is *His* life-energy. Our "work" is simply to receive it and allow God to be glorified as we bear much fruit from our union with Him. It's possible that entering into this process—this partnership—with God can be painful and trying as we shift from a position of self-effort to reliance on Him, but ultimately, as we emerge from the wrong perspective and converge with Jesus, our "burden [becomes] light" and our "yoke [becomes] easy."

> *The only "work" that is ultimately of any consequence or value in God's eyes is the finished work of the cross that only Jesus could perform*

Furthermore, the only "work" that is ultimately of any consequence or value in God's eyes is the finished work of the cross that only Jesus could perform: His sinless life of perfection, sacrificial and selfless death, and miraculous resurrection. It was for our benefit and reconciliation to the Father that Jesus did this and why it was Jesus alone who had to be the One to do it. We not only don't have to work for or earn the blessing; we can't and shouldn't. By doing so, we despise the perfection of God's perfect, once-and-for-all finished work.

Even in the Old Testament (of behavior-based Law), God graphically describes how offensive and disgusting this is to Him: "We are all like one who is unclean, all our so-called righteous acts are like a menstrual rag in your sight. We all wither like a leaf; our sins carry us away like the wind" (Isaiah 64:6 NET Bible). The Good News Translation of the same verse says it this way: "All of us have been sinful; even our best actions are filthy through and through. Because of our sins we are like leaves that wither and are blown away by the wind."

That's because without Jesus, even our very best fruit is rotten since it's connected to the wrong vine: the vine of sin and death because of separation from God. But under God's grace through the finished work of Jesus, even our very worst fruit is still pleasant to God because it's connected to the True Vine: the righteousness of God in Christ Jesus. As soon as we become born again, we are under His covenant of Grace; by *faith*. Romans 14:23 says that "Whatever is not from faith is sin." Our work is simply believing in and receiving His work. Everything else is just ineffective and misguided behavioral modification. As God told Pastor Joseph Prince: "*My* work... works. Your works... *don't* work!" Praise God for that!

Our work is simply believing in and receiving His work.

With all this being said, I wish I could tell you that I stayed in perfect peace and rock-solid faith throughout this entire season of seed-growing and fruit-bearing. Alas, that was not the case, but I trust that you can learn from my journey—from both my moments of victory and courage as well as my times of failure and fear.

CHAPTER 17

THE SEED IS IN THE GROUND (AND IT'S WORKING!)

It was Thursday, April 20, 2017. I had not had a revelation or felt this kind of life welling up within me for three or four years. This was when Charis has their annual "Campus Days" event, during which prospective students come to the Bible college for a week to get a sense of what life is like in that environment. During this time, Andrew Wommack (the President and Founder of Charis Bible College and Andrew Wommack Ministries) spoke about the Parable of the Sower from the Gospel of Mark, Chapter Four. I had heard this teaching countless times, but for some reason, this particular time there was a fresh revelation that totally rocked me. In that moment, the "logos" (written Word of God) became "rhema" (personal revelation within the heart that is supernaturally inspired by the Holy Spirit and "quickened," or brought to life, to our human spirit).

Before I share with you the revelation I heard from God, I want to back up for a bit to set the stage. You may be surprised by my admission at the end of the last chapter that, even after all the amazing things I just described, I was not in a place of perfect peace and sure faith the whole time. Many times when reading or hearing someone tell a powerful testimony, it's easy to lose a sense of the timeline through which that testimony happened. Typically, the testimonies are just highlights of the most important events and turning points in the lives of those sharing them. In order to be effective in maintaining the interest of the audience, the story is usually told with a sense of pacing that keeps things moving from one milestone to the next. The nuances of subtly skipping around in the timeline of the story can also be lost on the audience.

The hearer or listener hasn't personally lived the day-in, day-out mundane details of the chronological timeline between the important milestones (which is the vast majority of where we actually live our lives). Therefore, it can be easy to lose perspective of the impatience, frustration, and doubts experienced by the person who did live out that experience. This is especially true because you don't have the benefits of retrospect or knowledge of the outcomes to frame your perspective of things when you're in the middle of it. In addition, once we tell the story after the fact, we interpret things in light of what happened, which causes us to frame it in a certain way that may be very different from how we experienced it at the time. It's natural to put a positive spin on things after we've made it through the dry season and tasted the victory.

So, to put some more context into the telling of my story in the previous chapter, when I first got to Charis, I was really excited and expectant for what God was going to do in this new season. I met a lot of people I connected with when I first got there and really enjoyed going to class every day and having the "Charis experience." I've noticed that many times, at least for me, the inherent novelty of a major life shift can maintain a certain level of excitement for a period of time. But it's shocking to me how quick the "new car smell" of anything in life can wear off. I had experienced that phenomenon several times when I had first moved to Vail and then from Vail back to D.C.

The biggest struggle for me when I first moved back to Colorado to attend Charis was that I was not feeling like I had a really strong core group of friends. To start with, I was a "winter student," meaning that I started school in late November; I was joining a class of students who had mostly all started together in early September and generally had established their circles of friends. I'm a pretty outgoing person who tends to connect with people quickly and easily, and I did meet some very welcoming and great people right off the bat. But being a single 36-year-old (at the time) in a small mountain town, it was hard to find people I felt I could personally relate to. It seemed like most of them were either significantly older or younger than me. Those who were about my same age (mid-thirties at the time) usually had families.

Even for those people I did have a strong connection with, most of them were working a job and had to rush out right after school to get to work. I was planning on getting at least a part-time job when I first moved there, but I had enough VA benefits and passive income that I could live comfortably without one. I felt the Lord encourage me not to get a job so that I could devote all of my time and energy to receiving everything I possibly could from this season. This was certainly an extravagant blessing that most people didn't have, and for which I was extremely grateful.

But for a person like me, it can be hard to sit still for an extended period of time and just rest. Incidentally, I don't think it's a coincidence that God called someone like me to write a book on that very subject. I see this as analogous to how God transformed the most zealous legalist (Saul the Pharisee) to become the ultimate ambassador of pure grace (Paul the Apostle). You wouldn't think it would be very hard to enjoy oneself in a beautiful mountain town, going to a Spirit-filled Bible college, and *not* having to work a job. For me, though, the open schedule and abundant free time seemed to emphasize a sense of emptiness in general as well as a disconnect from people.

All that being said, I tried to make the most of the time I had. I woke up early every morning to pray, journal, and read the Bible. I eagerly attended class, diligently engaged with the material, attempted to ace every test, and gave my best in volunteer hours and other extracurricular activities. I was spending a lot of time, money, and effort working with a functional medicine doctor to improve my overall health through a holistic, natural approach. I attended church and got plugged in by serving there. All of these things were good, and I was gaining a lot from what I was learning in Bible college. But after a while, it just started to feel like an uphill battle, an endless grind that didn't seem to be moving the needle in any obvious way for me. I became frustrated at the experience and even resentful toward God. I would rant to Him and say things like, "I'm doing all this **work, trying** really **hard,** being obedient to do what *You* said to do, and it's getting me **nowhere!**" Lord, help me... will I never learn?!

Hopefully by now, you're seeing a fairly consistent theme throughout this book and my life: a cycle of self-effort, frustration, sometimes spectacular burnout or failure, repentance, resting and trusting in God, redemption, breakthrough, and then back to self-effort. Seemingly rinse and repeat. However, I've noticed that the cycles seem to be getting shorter and are generally forward and upward. Two steps forward, one step back. Two steps down, three steps up. And through it all, God is unfailingly gracious. He never gets angry or impatient. He doesn't smite us when we unload on Him with our whining and complaining. He always gently and lovingly corrects us by reminding us of the life-giving truth.

Even in those cases where His rebuke seems a little more sharp to me, it's *always* life-giving. He convicts me of doubting in His goodness and reminds me of all the times He's been faithful to me. He promises to deliver on what He's said and encourages me that I don't have to try to earn it. He warns me when I'm getting into the flesh, striving and toiling to bring something about by my own effort. He may not do it in my timing or in my way, but as it's said: "God is rarely early, but He's always on time." Again, with the benefit of retrospect, I now see that this period was a time of training in rest, patience, trust, and repentance of dependence on self to do anything of value for God.

One of the lines you hear repeatedly at Charis is, "Preparation time is never wasted time." I know that many years of seemingly wandering from place to place in an emotional and circumstantial wilderness has been preparation for me to speak about this message of grace and rest from a place of personal experience and overflow. All of these experiences were dove-tailing in some way or another from when I started school in November 2016 until April 2017. This period is when I got that revelation I mentioned at the beginning of the chapter listening to Andrew Wommack's message on Mark 4:1–20.

(At this point, please humor me as I appear to go down some theological and scientific rabbit holes; I promise to tie it all back together!)

To briefly summarize the Parable of the Sower, this passage is a metaphor explaining the process whereby the Word of God (the "seed") is sown into our hearts (the "soil") and has the potential to generate incredible results in our lives ("yields a crop"). The thing that determines whether or not we will get results and in what proportions is whether or not we believe God's Word in our *hearts*. It's one thing to *know* what God's Word says with our heads; it's an entirely different thing to truly *believe* what it says in our hearts. If we have unbelief, the Word gets choked because our heart is not fertile ground to let it work on our behalf. But if we accept the Word by coming into agreement with what it says, our hearts allow it to work for us and produce a supernaturally multiplied harvest of blessing in our lives and the lives of others.

Notice that the *Word* does the actual work, *not us*. We just provide it the right conditions to grow and flourish by believing it. It's worth noting that the "Word" of God is not just words on a page or information. In the natural realm, words are just a mutually agreed-upon structured arrangement of information to convey understanding. In the spiritual realm, words are a creative force that have the power to spiritually and physically manifest what is spoken and believed. Hebrews 4:12 tells us that the Word of God is *living* and *active*.

> *It's one thing to know what God's Word says with our heads; it's an entirely different thing to truly believe what it says in our hearts.*

The Strong's Concordance of the Greek word translated as "living" is "zao." Zao means that it is *literally* alive (not lifeless or dead). The Word of God literally carries the life of God Himself within it. In fact, **Jesus** *is* the Living Word that became flesh and dwelt among us. Therefore, it/He is able to produce and create life in the same way God created man and gave man the ability to create life. We create life not just biologically through our reproductive organs but spiritually by believing and speaking forth the Word of God. And *that* is our *only* work in the New Covenant of Grace: believing in Jesus (*The* Word) and the results

He/The Word can accomplish. He could not have made it more plain or simple than this:

> Then they asked him, "What must we do to do the works God requires?" Jesus answered, "The work of God is this: to believe in the one he has sent" (John 6:28–29).

Referring again to Hebrews 4:12, the Word of God is both "living" (zao) and *active*. The Strong's Concordance for the word transliterated to English as "active" is the Greek word "energés." "Energés" literally means *"energized, full of energy."* This is very interesting to me in light of how quantum physics works. Though I certainly am no expert myself, I have read enough about it to connect the dots between cutting-edge science and the ancient principles of my faith. (Two books on this subject that are both very fascinating and easily understandable are *The Physics of Heaven* by Ellyn Davis and Judy Franklin and *Quantum Faith* by Annette Capps).

Quantum physics seems to work in a completely different way from our traditional understanding of the known universe. In the quantum (infinitesimally small subatomic) realm, everything exists in the form of wavelengths, energy, and/or vibrations. In this realm, reality seems to exist only in the form of possibilities or probabilities. Somehow, the outcomes of those probabilities seem to be influenced by whether or not they are *observed*. What's even more bizarre is that the outcomes observed seem to be influenced by the specific observations or expectations of an individual observer. Unlike classical Newtonian physics, experimental results cannot be consistently repeated under otherwise identical conditions. It appears that our reality is much more "fluid" than science initially theorized.

Despite my parenthetical heads-up several paragraphs ago, by this point you may understandably be asking, *"Ryan, how does any of this relate to the story you were telling—and abruptly abandoned—about a personal revelation you had during Campus Days at Charis? And what does this have to do with God?!"* And the answer is: **everything!** You see, both science and the Word of God indicate that to a large extent *we create our own reality*. This happens as a result of what we expect and observe—in other words, what we *__believe__*.

Remember what Jesus said in the Parable of the Sower: If our hearts accept and receive the Word of God, it will work on our behalf as a seed planted in fertile ground that bears abundant fruit. The Word of God is

There is supernatural power in the Word of God.

alive and *full of energy* that vibrates at a specific frequency, which when coupled with the expectations and beliefs of the heart in which it's planted, can achieve a "harmonic resonance" of sorts that will physically manifest the promises the Word contains. Though I wasn't necessarily thinking of it in these exact terms at the time, I believe this was the process that started to unfold in my heart and life during Campus Days.

As Andrew was preaching on Mark 4, he talked about his own life and the early days of his ministry. For *years*, he didn't see any signs of progress or breakthrough. It was a very long, hard season for he and his wife Jamie. But he was absolutely convinced that what God had promised to him through His Word was true. Andrew used the analogy of being like a woman who has just recently become pregnant; though neither she nor anyone else can feel or see that she is pregnant, the "seed" is still growing inside her and will eventually become manifest if she just doesn't abort the pregnancy.

In some passages of scripture, the Greek word "sperma" is used to refer to the Word of God. And just like a sperm can impregnate a woman, we can become "pregnant" with the promises of God through His Word. Andrew emphasized that there *is* supernatural power in the Word of God. You have to *believe* that the seed is working beneath the ground when you *can't* see it, and not dig it up or abort it with unbelief. This is where God really started speaking to me, and I got that rhema word. I was furiously scribbling in my journal, trying to keep up with the deluge of revelation God was speaking to me:

> Ryan, this has been a year of sowing seed, building a foundation, and setting the groundwork. Stay with it; **the seed is in the ground, and it is working!** So much of your frustration right now is because you actually don't think anything is happening or being accomplished. Are you where I've led you? Are you doing the things I've said would help you? Have faith that it won't amount to nothing. It's actually that kind of thinking that can choke the Word and hinder you from the blessing. This is where you need to have faith. **Things are being accomplished and working on your behalf.**

This encouragement and belief that unseen and unfelt things were happening helped "prime the pump" in my heart to receive yet more words from God in the next few minutes and hours that would set my life on a new trajectory.

PERSONAL REFLECTION AND PRACTICAL APPLICATION

Are you believing God for His promises but frustrated from feeling like nothing is happening? Take heart! If you're believing and speaking it, God's Word is supernaturally active and powerfully working on your behalf. Hebrews 4:12 (AMPC) says, "For the Word that God speaks is alive and full of power [making it active, operative, energizing, and effective]..." John 6:29 makes it abundantly clear that our only work is to believe in Jesus (the Living Word). Be encouraged that, if you're believing God's Word in your heart, the seed is in the ground—and it's working!

CHAPTER 18

INVESTING IN GOD'S BEST

After Andrew finished up his message, a number of past and present Charis students shared their own testimonies of how they got to Charis and how God provided for them on that path. A strong theme I noticed running through all of them was financial lack and God giving them miracles of provision to get and keep them at Charis. While I thought this was really inspiring in some ways, I was also kind of discouraged that so many Spirit-filled believers committing their lives by coming to Bible college were even in that position in the first place.

What's even better than a miracle is continually living in God's blessing.

Andrew had just released a new book at the time called *Living in God's Best*. To paraphrase this book, Andrew shared about how it's *not* God's best for us to have to go from miracle to miracle because He's bailing us out of crisis after crisis. Because of God's unfailing patience and lovingkindness, He's always willing and able to do that for us. But what's even better than a miracle is continually living in God's *blessing*. When we're living in the blessing, we never even need a miracle to get us out of a jam because we're already "ahead of the curve." Instead of us constantly chasing after miracles to escape by the skin of our teeth, God's overtaking blessings are constantly chasing after *us*. To give a picture of what that can look like, here are a few examples:

- We don't need a miraculous *healing* because we're perpetually living in divine *health*.

- We don't need a financial miracle because we're living a life of *prosperity*.

- We don't need spiritual deliverance from demonic bondage because we're walking in *freedom*.

A hypothetical (but surprisingly representative) story from these student testimonies goes something like this: "I heard God call me to move to Colorado and go to Charis Bible College. But I didn't have any money in my bank account, I was sick, and I had no place to live when I got there. I didn't see any way to pay for rent or tuition. But somehow, I scrapped together enough funds through friends, family, and random checks in the mail to pack up and move to Colorado. I just barely rolled into town on fumes (because I couldn't pay for gas) and four bald tires. Then, I showed up to class registration not knowing how I was going to pay for the first tuition installment. Right as I was walking up to the desk to pay my tuition (which I didn't have the money for), out of nowhere, someone else in line paid my tuition for me because they felt like God told them to! Then, someone else offered to let me stay at their house rent-free! Every month until I graduated, somehow rent and tuition miraculously got paid. While I was in school, I had five demons cast out of me and received miraculous healing from a horribly painful, debilitating terminal prognosis for which the doctors gave me three months to live. But here I stand today, alive and well to tell all of you about it. ***Praise God!!!***"

184

I remember thinking to myself, *"Really?!"* Now, please don't get me wrong. I agree wholeheartedly that testimonies like this are undeniably miraculous. They showcase God's amazing faithfulness to do for us what is otherwise impossible without Him, through the supernatural power of the Gospel. And no doubt about it: God gets all the credit, honor, and glory for providing miracles like these. Also, I know we're all dealing with something (including me!), and I certainly don't mean to be insensitive or disparage anyone dealing with major challenges in their finances, health, or spiritual walk.

Christians should generally and consistently be the most prosperous, healthy, and functional members of society.

But it struck me as I heard one testimony after another like this (or something very similar) that, as awesome as these God stories are, I had to agree with Andrew that I certainly didn't think this was a demonstration of God's *best* for us. I started feeling the fire of a righteous anger inside of me about how so many members of the Body of Christ seemed to be the "tail" and not the "head." It was unacceptable to me.

I believe that as God's children and ambassadors to a watching world, we as Christians should generally and consistently be the *most* prosperous, healthy, and functional members of society. We should all be "conspicuously prominent" (from the Hebrew word "yatir") like the prophet Daniel, who had such undeniable wisdom, insight, health, excellence, and integrity that he stuck out like a sore thumb from everyone else around him. And most importantly of all, everyone who noticed this about Daniel *knew* it was because of his God. To *that*, I wholeheartedly say, **"Praise God!!!"**

After the student testimonies, the next session was by a woman named Carrie Pickett. Carrie had lived a life of seeing both the miracles as well as the blessings of God. Starting at this time, God was speaking to me things that I was writing down in my notes. As I was simultaneously listening to God and writing down what He said, I would hear something Carrie said that confirmed almost *verbatim* what God had *just* spoken to me! It was like a real-time stream of consciousness that was getting confirmed in real-time by what Carrie said. This happened several times over the course of the 50-minute message she shared. One example of this was when God told me, "If I give you something to do, it's My bill," which Carrie then said no later than I had just written it.

One of the things God was speaking to me about as I was taking notes and journaling during all this was finances; in particular, real estate investing. I had been sitting on a fairly large pile of cash that had accumulated over time and was being kept in my savings. I knew that this was not the best stewardship over this amount of resources. Investing in real estate had been on my mind for a while, but I just hadn't been able to find a suitable place to invest it that I felt comfortable with.

When I moved to Woodland Park, I saw and heard of the incredible economic growth the city had experienced in recent years. A significant factor for this was the influx of students and staff from Charis, since the college had relocated from Colorado Springs to Woodland Park in 2014. This caused an accelerated increase in property values and high demand for housing, especially in the local real estate rental market. I just assumed as a matter of course that if I were going to invest in real estate, it would be right here for a house that I lived in and rented out the other rooms to Charis students. That naturally also assumed (in my mind, at least) that I would do the "normal thing" and take out a loan to finance the home purchase, especially being eligible for a VA loan, which have very favorable interest rates and terms (such as 100% financing, where no money is required for a down payment).

But with my faith catalyzed so powerfully by Andrew's first message and now thinking about living in God's best, the Lord posed a question to me: "Do you have faith for me to give you a house or find one you can pay all cash for? Getting a mortgage loan/debt isn't a sin, but don't limit Me with your small thinking and box Me in with uncontested false assumptions." **Right then,** Carrie said the following:

> If your vision can be accomplished without supernatural help, it's too small. Don't look at your life and figure out, "How am I gonna do it?" Don't do it out of your own strength and wisdom; that's stupid. You say, "that's impossible" in your own limited thinking, and in and of yourself that's true. But when you start believing and depending on God… whew! God *wants* us to be bearing *supernatural* fruit and is glorified by this. God did not call you to live an ordinary, natural, limited life but a Spirit-led one of overflow. Don't plan your own life. It *has* to be God; it *has* to be that divine overflow.

Wow! How 'bout a little o' *that* for some timely divine confirmation?! It really was totally beyond me to grasp how I could possibly afford to buy an all-cash investment property, but I was now at least willing to entertain the thought. The next day, I was contemplating this as Andrew was giving another message on living in God's best and not settling for anything less. In my notes, I wrote down the following question: "Don't settle for having to get a mortgage?" Literally at the exact moment I had finished writing the last word in that sentence, Andrew mentioned not going in debt! "Don't tolerate less than God's best," he said. He then shared a testimony of an earlier time when the ministry had been able to purchase a $3.2 million property debt-free! Beyond that, I knew that the current property and buildings I was sitting in at the time had been paid for without any debt at all, to the tune of $75 million. And that project was started smack-dab in the depths of the financial crisis in 2008 to 2009!

I know God is no respecter of persons, and if He could do it for Andrew, then He could do it for me. So I started praying about this in earnest: for the right people and the right investment opportunities to come into my life at the right time. I started speaking with different people about it, and several months later, I was referred by a friend to someone named "Bob." Bob bought his first house at the age of 18 and had since built a large portfolio of investment properties. He had just finished his second year at Charis and was working for the ministry and had helped several people in the community buy investment properties.

I met with Bob, and he shared with me his approach. Before he came to Charis, he had been in a relatively senior position at a major bank. This, combined with his real estate investment experience, gave him great experience in assessing certain markets. He explained to me how he uses a "top-down" analysis, meaning that he looks at a variety of data points on a national level to determine the best city or area to invest in. Based on his analysis, he decided to invest in Columbus, Ohio, instead of Woodland Park or Colorado Springs. This was a completely different way of thinking about it than I had ever heard.

Columbus had a lot of the characteristics he was looking for from a real estate investment standpoint: strong population growth, diversified employment sectors (meaning that if one industry was negatively affected, like the auto industry in Detroit, the whole town doesn't go down with it), a number of universities and colleges attracting young talent, a "straight line" economy (where homes prices are very stable over time, making them more immune to large-scale downturns or recessions). Perhaps one of the more important factors about Columbus properties is that the ratio between the purchase price and rent allowed for high monthly cashflow with a relatively low up-front capital investment. This was especially important to me as an all-cash investor. In fact, most of his purchases and those of his clients were on an all-cash basis. This allows one more negotiating leverage as a buyer because it is much faster and simpler to close a deal, making cash offers more attractive to sellers.

He had a trip scheduled in the next few weeks with a number of potential investors he takes to different areas of the city to show them a list of properties that fit his criteria. He had a team established that he had used for his own investments consisting of a realtor, property management company, and a contractor. I quickly learned that having existing relationships with a trusted team like this is critical for any investor and especially for out-of-state investors who will be absentee landlords. I booked a flight to attend this investor trip, and we looked at about 30 to 40 properties over two days. It was a huge learning curve for me, but going in, I had a fairly good general idea of what I was looking for in an investment property. My biggest priority was something that would give me a high passive monthly income I could live on at a price I could pay all cash for with enough extra margin for unexpected expenses.

When I first arrived in Woodland Park (thinking at the time that I would be buying there), the Lord spoke to me that when I had a specific idea in mind of what I was looking for, I would recognize the right property almost as soon as I walked in the door. It would be a clear confirmation of what was already in my mind and heart. The first day on the Columbus trip, we looked at about 15 to 20 properties. Some of them had great potential, but nothing was clearly highlighted to me. The second day, we looked at several in the morning, but halfway through that day, I saw one that really stuck out to me. As soon as we walked in the door to look at the property, I got the sense that this could be "the one."

It was a nice, all-brick multifamily quadruplex (or "4plex") consisting of four individual two-bedroom, one-bathroom apartments. Each apartment unit was about 1,000 square feet and had two stories. Three of the four units had been "gutted" and completely rehabbed within the last six months or so. It was in a decent area of the city but was on a rough street. Because of that, it was much cheaper than comparable buildings would be. It was listed at $140,000, and between the four units, it brought in a total of about $2,750 of total rent! For anyone who doesn't study real estate investment, that is an *incredible* price-to-rent ratio. One rule of thumb in real estate is to look for properties that have a ratio of 1% of monthly income to purchase price. For example, this would be a property that generates $1,000 of monthly income for a purchase price of $100,000. If you do the math, you'll see that this property had a ratio of more than *double* that!

These ratios are very difficult to achieve in a low-interest rate environment, where the average person has low cost of capital and can increase their purchasing power through low interest rates. It's even harder to hit those ratios when it's also a strong seller's market with a lot of buyer demand. Both of those conditions (low interest rates in a strong seller's market) were present in this case, which is what makes this all the more amazing. This particular property was already under contract, but we had some valuable insight because the listing agent was the realtor Bob worked with (who accompanied us on the trip). Apparently, the financing contingency for the buyer's loan was in jeopardy of falling through, and the seller (her client as the listing agent) needed to close quickly to cash out and reinvest into another project. So a cash offer would definitely help him out in this situation.

Bob and I worked the numbers, and he thought, based on this situation, that I could get the property for quite a bit less than the listing price of $140k, which would increase my returns that much more. After a *lot* of talking, praying, and analyzing a ton of numbers, I submitted a backup offer to the existing primary offer for a little over $120,000. Shortly thereafter, the primary offer fell through because of the buyer's financing contingency. After negotiating back and forth with the seller for about a week with several counteroffers, my backup offer became the primary, and we were under contract for a sales price of a little over $125,000. Between my savings, cash value in a life insurance policy, and cashing out a lower-yielding portion of my financial investment portfolio, I was able to come up with enough cash for the purchase, with enough extra margin to make me feel comfortable.

With everything in order, a total of only *two weeks* after making the trip to Columbus, we closed the deal. I was now officially the owner of an investment property several states away that was generating a **gross annual return of over 25%,** and the best part is that I was able to pay for it **without using debt of any kind!** My head was spinning. I couldn't believe this actually just happened! To generate that kind of gross income from a house in Woodland Park, very conservatively it probably would have cost me at least $400,000 and would have been impossible to do on an all-cash basis. But... God!

I should add that, as someone who has a fairly strong grasp of finance and investments, it makes absolutely no logical sense to buy an investment property for cash. One of the things you'll often hear people in real estate talk about is the magic of "leverage" (debt) and "OPM" (Other People's Money) to accelerate the wealth-building process. Debt allows you to stretch the value of your own money much further by acquiring more properties, more quickly. It's also much more tax-efficient, since the interest on the loan is tax-deductible. By all rights, I'll be the first one to admit that buying a property all-cash is an extremely inefficient use of investment capital. This is especially true of someone like myself who does not have a large net worth and is relatively limited in my ability to continue growing my investment portfolio.

However, as I frequently quote from 1 Corinthians 1:25, "the foolishness of God is greater than human wisdom, and the weakness of God is greater than human strength." On a practical note, I now see God's wisdom in not using debt to purchase a property in this specific instance. Because I was a cash buyer, I did not have a loan financing contingency. That was the reason that I was able to get this property under contract from the seller, because of the time-sensitive nature of the situation. Additionally, it allowed me to buy the property at a discount to what other buyers using financing probably would have gotten it for. This served to increase my returns and lower my risk by lowering my price point. As the old saying goes: "You make money when you buy, not when you sell." The tagline of A Better Way's podcast is "Where the Supernatural Meets the Practical." I believe there is always eventually a practical aspect to doing business and life through the supernatural power and guidance of the Holy Spirit, no matter how crazy it seems.

"The wisdom of God is greater than human wisdom, and the weakness of God is greater than human strength."

Moreover, going back to that word God spoke to me through Andrew, Carrie, and others during Campus Days at Charis, I *knew* that this was God's blessing because I did it *His* way. The Lord invited me into an opportunity to challenge Him for His best in asking and believing Him for something that seemed utterly impossible to me at the time (an all-cash property purchase). Through this experience, He was proving to me (and hopefully also to you as the reader) that what is impossible for man is easy for God! By submitting to the counterintuitive and countercultural leading of the Holy Spirit, I have investment results and am now living a life that *demands* a supernatural explanation.

When we are willing to start believing and depending on God, over-the-top blessings and outcomes are possible!

Like Andrew said, we should not tolerate anything less than God's *best* for our lives. And as Carrie also said during Campus Days, if our vision can be accomplished without supernatural help from God, it's *too small*. God doesn't want us to do anything out of our own limited human strength and wisdom. He doesn't want us to be living an ordinary life, but rather a life of Spirit-led overflow that *has* to point to *Him*. When we are willing to start believing and depending on *God*, over-the-top blessings and outcomes are possible!

What's even more, everything I've shared so far about this particular testimony is only *half* the story, as we'll learn about more in future chapters...

PERSONAL REFLECTION AND PRACTICAL APPLICATION

Ask God for His absolute <u>best</u> for you in a *specific* area of your life. Invite the Holy Spirit to challenge your current thinking and increase your faith about finances, investments, business, or something else by giving you a new idea or decision-making process. Then, share your testimonies to inspire and encourage someone else! You can go to https://abetterwaypodcast.com/nominations to do so through the podcast.

CHAPTER 19

DIVINE APPOINTMENTS AND KAIROS MOMENTS

I've noticed throughout my life and the lives of others, particularly in scripture, that there are times when things tend to happen all at once. We may feel like we're on a never-ending uphill march with no visible progress or end in sight, when suddenly there seem to be a series of positive events that rapidly converge in a brief timespan. I refer to these as "kairos" or "God-opportune" moments.

"Kairos" is a Greek word meaning the right, critical, or opportune moment. The ancient Greeks had two words for time: chronos and kairos. The former refers to chronological or sequential time, while the latter signifies a proper or opportune time for action. God's Kingdom seems to work on more of an exponential, rather than linear, scale. The line on the graph seems to be very flat for a long time until it reaches an inflection point of a steep upward trajectory in the curve. This was the case for me during the week I was about to close the deal on that investment property.

In September of 2017, I did a podcast interview with a couple from my class in Bible college named Johnny and

Jeanie Rhodes, who shared a powerfully moving testimony (which you can listen to on podcast episode ABW 9 - The Power of the Father's Love, Part 1). We developed a close personal connection through that conversation, which led to unexpected opportunities and important relationships. A couple days after the podcast interview, Johnny called me about a "unique opportunity."

He told me the ministry occasionally uses student volunteers as drivers for visiting VIP guests while they're in town. He had just been asked by Joan, the ministry's Hospitality Coordinator, if he knew of anyone that would be a good fit. Because of our recent conversation, Johnny said I immediately came to mind. In order to be available for up to a week at a time to accommodate these VIPs, one of the requirements was that these students **not have a job**. (Recall the struggle I initially had about submitting to God's leading for me not to get a job when I first came to Charis; we'll circle back to later in this chapter.)

Johnny put me in contact with the Hospitality Coordinator, and she felt comfortable enough after our meeting to offer me the role for an upcoming event. The VIPs to whom I was assigned were Pastor Jerome ("PJ") Fernandez from Sri Lanka and his head of security, Praveen. I had never heard of Pastor Jerome before, but he and

Jesus is expressed in such beautiful diversity through all nations, peoples, tribes, and tongues throughout the whole earth.

Praveen were both an absolute pleasure to work for. In their own ways, each of them projected an almost tangible humility, gentleness, excellence, generosity, and truly powerful spiritual depth. I was particularly struck by the manner in which their cultural background expressed those Christ-like qualities in a unique and different way than I was used to seeing at Charis. It was a picture to me of how Jesus is expressed in such beautiful diversity through all nations, peoples, tribes, and tongues throughout the whole earth.

This unique cultural difference was powerfully evident during Pastor Jerome's sessions at the conference. Like me, most people in attendance had not heard of him before, but I don't think a single person there would deny that he was the highlight of the conference. Every person I talked to who was there could undeniably feel the manifest presence of the Holy Spirit as He ministered through Pastor Jerome. PJ has a very unique prophetic gift, which he activates by singing in the Spirit, or tongues. Even though by this point I was very familiar with seeing and operating in a variety of supernatural and prophetic gifts, I had never seen it expressed in quite this way before. At first, it seemed kind of odd, even weird, to me and others.

But once again, this demonstrates how God's ways so often go contrary to our "carnal" (natural, human) ways of thinking. His wisdom is not of this world; that's because it *transcends it!* In living color, through personal and experiential knowledge, this brought the Word of God to life for me in a new way (Ephesians 5:16–19 NKJV, my emphasis):

> *See then that you walk circumspectly, not as fools but as wise, redeeming the time, because the days are evil. Therefore do not be unwise, but understand what the will of the Lord is.* ***And do not be drunk with wine, in which is dissipation; but be filled with the Spirit, speaking to one another in psalms and hymns and spiritual songs, singing and making melody in your heart to the Lord.***

Having created this atmosphere through singing in the Spirit, Pastor Jerome would receive a very specific and accurate "word of knowledge" or "word of wisdom" from the Holy Spirit. 1 Corinthians 12:8 (NLT) says, "To one person the Spirit gives the ability to give wise advice; to another the same Spirit gives a message of special knowledge." He would then release this "word" to a specific individual in the crowd God wanted to speak to about something personally. One after the other, he'd give these personal words to several different people—most or all of whom he didn't know anything about at all—about something Pastor Jerome could not possibly have known himself. Their responses made it quite clear this was indeed the Holy Spirit Himself speaking and ministering deeply into their hearts. And, referring to Ephesians 5:18, there was almost a sense of being "intoxicated" by the tangible power and presence of God.

I was so honored to have had the privilege to serve this humble yet powerfully anointed man of God. Through PJ and Praveen, I was experiencing Jesus in a new way that was both inspiring and convicting. They manifested aspects of His character in some ways that I do not but would very much like to. The three of us had a great rapport, and it ended up being a connection deeper than just a job. Overall, it was a great experience, and things went really well for everyone involved. As I mentioned before, this was also the week that I closed on the property. Harvests seem to come in "batches" sometimes, and it wasn't over yet!

The next week at school, I saw a poster for that year's "Men's Advance," an annual men's conference hosted at Charis, for which NFL Coach Tony Dungy would be one of the guest speakers. I sent up a brief prayer: "God, not a huge deal either way, but it would be really cool if I could be Tony's driver for that." But I resolved that I would not ask anyone about it, considering that God was clearly capable and willing to bring that opportunity to me if it was His best.

This is something I'm frequently convicted about, because my natural tendency is to try to *make* things happen if I really want them to. This "go-getter" attitude is celebrated in our culture, and many times gets results. But I am now learning a *better* way, which is to pray and wait on *God* to bring things to *me*—in *His* timing—instead of chasing after them myself. In my experience, this self-focused striving tends to either repel people and opportunities or get me into situations that end up not being good. **Sometimes, getting what you want is worse than not getting it,** (for those who have ears to hear). I'm by no means perfect at this, but I now at least consciously try to rest and wait on God to bring me what I desire, trusting that if I'm being led by the Spirit and it doesn't happen, then that's probably a *good* thing.

Within a couple days of seeing the poster of Tony Dungy and praying that prayer, a staff member walked up to me and asked if I was going to be driving for the men's conference. I said no one had talked to me about it yet but that I was more than willing

> *God uses divine appointments with people to accomplish His purposes*

to if they wanted me. As if she were feeling bad about making an unreasonable request, she almost sheepishly asked me if I would be willing to drive for Tony Dungy or James Brown. I laughed and assured her in no uncertain terms that I would be *thrilled* to do so! I could've sworn she seemed visibly relieved.

God uses divine appointments with people to accomplish His purposes, and I believe Tony Dungy was one of the divine appointments God had for me. For starters, Coach Dungy is one of the finest role models I've ever seen, let alone personally met. There is not an ounce of conceit, pride, or self-preoccupation with him. As an example, he traveled by himself with one small bag to the Colorado Springs regional airport where I picked him up. No entourage, no private jet, not even a personal assistant! He is a man who truly puts God first and lives an exemplary life for others to emulate.

Coach Dungy has trusted God and been true to himself when it really mattered, rejecting prevailing worldly opinion, even when it cost him dearly. One of his dreams was to become an NFL Head Coach, but it seemed like he was never going to get there. He was already on an uneven playing field as an African American, but he shared how he wouldn't scream and curse as other NFL coaches did to try to get results. Everyone told him he'd never make it with his calm, reserved coaching style, but he steadfastly refused to be someone he wasn't and trusted God to lead and guide him in the way in which *he* should go.

Eventually, doing things God's way paid off, and he became head coach for the Tampa Bay Buccaneers. Even then, he had to face tremendous setback and disappointment when he got fired after leading the Bucs through a miraculous turnaround and getting to the playoffs. He also endured the heartbreaking loss of his son in 2005 but never questioned his faith in God. In 2006 with the Indianapolis Colts, Coach Dungy became the first African-American Head Coach in NFL history to lead his team to a Super Bowl victory. He wrote about this journey in his book, *Quiet Strength*.

It was his testimony of publishing that book that most caught my attention, because it demonstrates so well the message of *A Better Way*. After winning the Super Bowl, he finally decided to write a book with his friend Nathan Whitaker. Nathan was a fellow brother in Christ on the administrative staff in Tampa Bay who had been asking Coach for years to write a book together. He encouraged Tony to use his platform to make an impact for Jesus through this book, but Coach was never interested. Following the momentum of the recent Super Bowl victory, though, Coach was open to doing it.

Tony and Nathan went to several publishers to talk about this. All the major publishers, marketing specialists, and public relations people gave Tony their advice on publishing and launching a book. They all said he needed to do the following to make this happen successfully:

- Take a whole year off to do extensive writing, editing, marketing, and book tours,
- Go through a major international publishing house in New York City,
- Work with a well-known, professional published author,
- Narrow his scope to a well-defined target market, focused on sports versus faith.

But Tony had already given the Colts his word to coach the following year. He also was committed to working with Nathan, who had never published a book before. They wanted to use Coach Dungy's personal story and faith as a central aspect of the book so that it could speak to people beyond just the sports market. He had a really tight timeline to finish the book before the next season started. So, despite all of the advice from experts, he did the following:

- Wrote the entire book in six *weeks,*
- Published through a small Christian publishing company based in the Midwest,
- Wrote it with a completely unknown and unpublished author (Nathan),
- Wrote it to a general market, emphasizing his faith along with football.

All of the experts said that, using this approach, he would be lucky to sell about 75,000 copies of the book. Consistent with his lifelong pattern of not allowing the world to force him into its mold, Coach Dungy followed what he felt was God's way in doing this, for His glory. The results are nothing short of remarkable, and speak for themselves:

- Over 1.5 *million* copies sold.
- It was the first-ever sports book to make the #1 New York Times bestseller list.
- It has now had at least six printings.
- Perhaps most importantly, many people have told Coach Dungy how meaningfully the book impacted their life because of all that he shared about his faith and personal story.

What a perfect example of 1 Corinthians 1:25: "God's foolishness being wiser than human wisdom, and God's weakness being stronger than human strength." He did everything exactly *opposite* to what all the foremost experts said and achieved success and impact "exceedingly, abundantly beyond all that you could ask, think, or imagine!" Tony Dungy has now published 17 books.

Of course, as I heard all this, I couldn't help but earnestly desire to share this through a podcast testimony. However, I had made the decision that I didn't want to even appear to be using my position for self-promotion. Once again, I prayed and asked God to open the door to an interview with Coach Dungy without having to ask for it. Silently praying for God to open doors seemed to have worked pretty well recently. In this instance, it would pay off yet again.

He did everything exactly opposite to what all the foremost experts said and achieved success and impact "exceedingly, abundantly beyond all that you could ask, think, or imagine!"

I had now become the ministry's "go-to" driver for VIPs, and about five months after driving Tony, I was asked to drive James Brown. James, who goes by "JB," is an Emmy-award-winning sports network broadcaster who has been at the top of his game for decades. If you've been even a casual observer of NFL football for the past 20+ years, you've probably seen him announcing games. JB is extremely close friends with Tony and had previously been a keynote speaker at Men's Advance. It was now August 2018, and James was coming out for a few days to record a show with Andrew Wommack.

JB is one of the most personable guys I've ever met, and we immediately hit it off. Everything I said about Coach Dungy's character and faith I found to be equally true of JB. I could immediately see why they were so close. Whereas Coach Dungy exudes quiet strength and calmness, JB is a quintessential high-energy extrovert. Everywhere I took him, whether in the VIP "Green Room" at Charis or at the grocery store in town, James would strike up a conversation with anyone and everyone. I jokingly started calling him "The Mayor" because of the way he was always "campaigning" everywhere he went.

JB was genuinely interested in getting to know me and was always asking questions about any topic that interested either of us. As fellow high-energy extroverts and wordsmiths, we had some very engaging conversations. He quickly learned about the podcast and that I was Tony's driver last time. When I described Tony's testimony of the book release and how perfectly it aligned with the theme of *A Better Way*, he asked if I had interviewed him. I told him why I hadn't, and he reached out to Coach right then to ask him to do it. Tony responded shortly to say that he would be *happy* to. I couldn't believe it; I now had an interview set up with Tony Dungy! (You can listen to it on podcast episode ABW 15 - Uncommon Success with Tony Dungy.)

James really took a liking to me and would be doing his Mayor campaign routine, introducing and promoting me to people everywhere we went. Learning of my military service, he began referring to me as "Lieutenant Ryan," which I then became jokingly known as to many people at school and the ministry. I've since driven him and Tony several more times, and we've continued to deepen our friendship and rapport.

I found it interesting that despite being a consummate professional at the highest levels of network broadcasting, James mentioned that he still can get really nervous before going live. I don't know why, though, since every time I've seen him speak he brings the house down with flawless content and delivery. He was particularly nervous before one speech on this trip, and I felt the Holy Spirit nudge me to give him a quick word of encouragement right before he went on. Something a mentor of mine once said came to my mind, which I shared with him: "If you're nervous, it's because you're more focused on performing than contributing." I encouraged James that he was a contributor to everyone here and that we couldn't wait to be blessed by what God was going to share with us through him.

He was very moved by that, and of course, he absolutely *crushed* it. He finished to a standing ovation and a deafening roar from over a thousand men, including me. After that, he started calling me his "security blanket" and would make special requests to Guest Services

> *"If you're nervous, it's because you're more focused on performing than contributing."*

that I be allowed with him into the green room backstage or on the set in the production studio. (As a general rule, no one is allowed in those areas unless they're a VIP guest, top-level leadership, or otherwise essential personnel.)

Again, my goal for this whole book is simply to brag on Jesus and His grace to do for us what we can't (or wouldn't) do for ourselves. In Matthew 23:12, Jesus says, "And whoever exalts himself will be humbled, and he who humbles himself will be exalted." By humbling myself and putting things in God's hands through prayer and simple steps of trust and faith, *He* promoted me and positioned me for increase. He will do the same for you!

One of the most significant ways God does this is through "divine appointments" (relationships and connections with people) and "kairos," or "God-opportune" moments. As I've heard it said many times, trust moves at the speed of relationship, and "it's not what you know but who you know." We allow these God-opportune moments to come to us when we cease striving in our own strength and effort by resting in God and asking Him to open the doors. This is what I've tried to demonstrate through this chapter.

Circling back to what I said earlier in the chapter about resting and not getting a job: although at first reluctant, I went against my own carnal thinking and continued to follow God's invitation to "invest in rest." By not seeking employment, I could spend my time getting the most out of my experience at Bible college, and in doing so, I made myself available for whatever God had for me. By submitting myself to the "foolishness" and "weakness" of God (1 Corinthians 1:25), He helped me to be more productive in what *He* was calling me to and opened doors of opportunity I wouldn't otherwise have had. It made me eligible to be a volunteer driver, which led to divine appointments and opened doors. *By putting me in a place of rest, God was actually positioning me for increase.*

"Resting in God" does *not* mean being passive or unproductive, though. In a sense, I was working a full-time job by investing in my time with God and following His leading and guidance. As mentioned in a previous chapter, it's amazing how the simplest and smallest steps of trust and obedience on our part lead to God doing big things for us on His part. Case in point: One of the reasons Johnny thought of me when Joan asked him about volunteer drivers is because he felt it could help expand the influence

Small, simple steps of obedience led to divine appointments, favor, and unanticipated God opportunities.

and message of *A Better Way*, which he now really believed in because of our interview. Taking that first small step of faith when I initially came to Charis led to the podcast, which led to my interview with Johnny and Jeanie, which then led to being a driver for VIPs and all the divine appointments following this opportunity.

Small, simple steps of obedience led to divine appointments, favor, and unanticipated God opportunities. This happened in a way *I* never could have expected or planned myself. Jeremiah 10:23 says, "I know, LORD, that our lives are not our own. We are not able to plan our own course." But God is! This always brings the glory back to Him as a witness and testimony for others to know Him and His goodness in a deeper way.

PERSONAL REFLECTION AND PRACTICAL APPLICATION

Instead of chasing after relationships and opportunities in your own strength—whether it's for your business, ministry, or personal life—try this as a prayerful experiment: ask God to intersect your path with the right people, at the right place, at the right time, for the right reasons. Spend more time praying and talking to God about it than you do with other people. Ask the Holy Spirit to clearly show you those divine appointments as they come into your life, and then *continue* to be Spirit-led as you walk that process out.

CHAPTER 20

GRACE IS DIVINE EMPOWERMENT

One criticism that so-called "radical grace" teachers and proponents endure is that their message will make people become "slack" on the topic of sinful versus right living. These critics believe an over-emphasis on grace will cause people to abuse God's grace as a license to sin. First, I'd like to borrow a quote from Andrew Wommack and jokingly say, "You need a license for that?!" The point being, most people will justify their own sin and error whether or not God's pure, unmixed grace is being taught.

I believe these critics of "excessive" grace are well-meaning but deceived about the true nature of grace. They think God's grace needs to be "balanced" with "our part," which is essentially us doing something to earn or deserve the grace we've been given. As Joseph Prince says, "What man calls 'balance' God calls 'mixture,' and God is not about mixture." Human "doing" to earn God's blessing is actually the basis of the Old Covenant law.

We cannot mix Old and New Covenants and expect to benefit from either. It sounds really good—even holy or honoring to

God—to think that we need to "give back" or "earn" the amazing gift of grace He's given us. But such a belief reveals a fundamental lack of understanding: God's grace, by its very definition, is something that cannot and will not be earned

The life God calls us to live as His ambassadors and saints is not difficult; it's impossible!

by any human effort. We actually insult the cross and negate God's grace by trying to add to it.

It's so important that we realize it is not by our own legalistic human striving and effort that we can exhibit godly excellence and integrity in our business and personal lives but by God's grace *alone*. The life God calls us to live as His ambassadors and saints is not difficult; it's *impossible!* Matthew 19:23–26 (AMP) makes this clear:

> Jesus said to His disciples, "I assure you *and* most solemnly say to you, it is difficult for a rich man [who clings to possessions and status as security] to enter the kingdom of heaven. Again I tell you, it is easier for a camel to go through the eye of a needle than for a rich man [who places his faith in wealth and status] to enter the kingdom of God." When the disciples heard this, they were completely astonished *and* bewildered, saying, "Then who can be saved [from the wrath of God]?" But Jesus looked at them and said, "With people [as far as it depends on them] it is impossible, but with God all things are possible."

God's grace is not getting what you deserve (punishment for our sin) and getting what you do not deserve (unmerited favor and blessings we did nothing to earn). This is absolutely true, both in my personal experience as well as scripturally. I shared at the beginning of this book how, by God's grace alone, I have been spared the pain and consequences of my sin and unwise decisions. I have also received rewards and blessings I very clearly did not earn or deserve.

But there's another aspect of God's grace that many people seem to be ignorant of or disregard: **divine empowerment to live a godly life.** The Apostle Paul was a perfect example of this: "But whatever I am now, it is all because God poured out his special favor on me—**and not without results. For I have *worked harder* than any of the other apostles; yet it was *not I* but *God* who was working *through* me by his <u>grace</u>.**" (1 Corinthians 15:10 NLT, emphasis mine). God's grace not only superabounds (exceeds)

Anyone who uses God's grace to justify sin, laziness, or anything else unbecoming of Jesus has not taken grace too far, but rather, not far enough.

our sin and failure but our human abilities as well. When God's grace is mixed with our belief and receipt, it supercharges our output. Another little gem from Andrew Wommack is this: "You'll live better accidentally under Grace than you ever did on purpose under the Law."

Anyone who uses God's grace to justify sin, laziness, or anything else unbecoming of Jesus has not taken grace too far, but rather, not far *enough.* In order for grace to work for you and bear good fruit in your life, you can't stay in the shallow end of the pool or go halfway with it. You have to plumb the depths of God's grace to benefit from it the way He designed you to. Perhaps a scientific metaphor will help illustrate this better than I can explain it.

In certain parts of the ocean, there is actually more oxygen at lower depths. Using a hypothetical but representative scenario, in a specific area of the world, the surface water may contain 30% of normal oxygen levels. Twenty feet down, it may be 20%. Forty feet down, the water may only contain 10% of normal oxygen levels. But *100 feet down*, it may have 100% oxygen. If you were running out of air and suffocating, even though it may seem counterintuitive and very scary, you'd be much better off diving deeper in order to get to the oxygen-rich area. The *worst* thing you could do would be to dive only halfway, though. If God's grace is the oxygen we need to stay alive (and I believe it is!), it's not the people who go too far with it who run into problems but the people who only go halfway.

There was a time in my life when I experienced this powerfully. It was when I was in the Vail Valley in 2016. Despite everything in my past, I had started drinking recreationally again about two years before that. As I should have expected, there were still times I struggled to moderate my drinking and had way too much. One night around April of 2016, I got so drunk I completely blacked out and didn't remember anything past about 10 p.m. I woke up the next day with a terrible hangover but feeling even worse because of embarrassment, guilt, and shame from losing control like that. I would be driving my car on my way to visit a friend of mine who lived over an hour away.

Technically, even though it had been about 12 hours since I'd had anything to drink, I probably should not have been driving since I was still kind of drunk from the night before. I knew full well how many bullets I had dodged in my life up until that point because of drinking, and I couldn't believe I was doing it to such excess again. My brokenness and shame were overwhelming me, and I made no attempt to deny or justify them. But in that moment as I was hungover, driving my car to visit my friend, I heard the gentle voice of the Holy Spirit speak to me: "Let Me love you through this, Ryan."

That sweet gentleness of the Holy Spirit broke something inside me, and I immediately lost it. Tears were streaming down my face as the Holy Spirit showered me in God's love and grace at a time I felt the least worthy of either. And it was the *depth* of that love and grace that actually empowered me to stop the cycle once again. I could have received God's grace and love "halfway" and known very truly that I could keep drinking and God would keep loving me. He could even keep sheltering me from the consequences of my bad decisions on an ongoing basis as He had before.

But the depth of acceptance, love, and grace in that moment was enough to overpower the brokenness driving me to continue to drink and gave me the desire and strength to quit once again. God not only gives us His will and purpose for our lives in a way that is pleasing to Him, but He also puts within us the desire, energy, and strength to do it. As the True Vine giving nutrients to the branches, it is the life energy of God Himself that empowers and energizes us to live with excellence, integrity, love, service, and selflessness for others.

> *It is the life energy of God Himself that empowers and energizes us to live with excellence, integrity, love, service, and selflessness for others.*

Therefore, to be quite frank, something that really bothers me about many so-called "Kingdom business" people, companies, and organizations is their disturbing lack of excellence, integrity, and generosity. I hate to say it, but many times co-called Christians are the absolute *worst* in business! It seems like the louder and more boldly they talk about their faith, the more difficult to deal with and dishonorable they are. If your primary "unique value proposition" as a businessperson is "I'm a Christian!" it's probably because you're *weak* in other areas of your business! You might say, "Hey, that's harsh! After all, isn't this supposed to be a book about God's grace?!" Yes, it is! And I don't mean to be harsh or condemning. I just want to make sure we're clear about what God's grace *actually is* and how it looks in practical application.

God's grace should give us more energy, higher standards, greater integrity, surpassing excellence, and unparalleled service to add more value than any other business or person. Like the Apostle Paul, God's grace should divinely empower us to work harder and get us better results than anyone else in our fields. You may be asking, "Isn't this a book about rest?" Once again, yes!

When we are resting in God's awesome grace and abilities instead of our own, He gives us the ability and desire to represent Him as He truly is to those around us. Even (and especially) when that appears at first glance to be difficult, His promise is true: "My grace is sufficient for you, for My strength is made perfect in weakness" (2 Corinthians 12:9). Our humble awareness and acknowledgement of our own weakness, inability, and even unwillingness sets us up to receive His superabundant grace to do what we can't do on our own.

God's grace not only gives us mercy and unmerited favor but divinely empowers us to reach the high calling He's given us. This is why I chafe so much when I see people misrepresenting God's grace in business and ministry through stinginess, mediocrity, dysfunction, and shady dealings. If you are a Christian, you have Jesus living inside you, in your spirit that is born from above. With Him comes divine empowerment to be world-class businesspeople of excellence, integrity, generosity, wisdom, and cultural impact. In other words: God's *best*! His divine empowerment also gives us patience and longsuffering to endure seasons of contradiction, setbacks, and disappointment so that we don't give up on the way to seizing the prize of that high calling.

A pastor friend of mine once told me, **"The Law demands, but Grace supplies."** This is true not only of salvation and our eternal security but of everything we need to live our lives on this earth to represent the true nature of God and His Kingdom.

On the road of grace, people often seem to be in one of two opposite ditches: sinful carnality or religious legalism. The former is embracing "grace" in order to justify sin and laziness. The latter is rejecting grace by trying to live a life of excellence and "godliness" from self-effort. In both cases, it's all flesh and no spirit; in neither case is it Christ-like. At different times of my life, I've found myself in both ditches.

If you're finding yourself in either of these ditches, no matter what side of the road you're on, my response is the same: You haven't yet plumbed the depths and riches of God's grace. As you go deeper and further into the ocean of God's grace, you'll experience *His* resultant power that is released within you and comes through you but is not *from* you. A revelation of God's grace releases supernatural power that will give you victory over sin and dysfunction in a way that self-effort and willpower never could. God's grace will energize you to live a godly life of integrity, excellence, diligence, drive, and perseverance as well as joy, peace, mercy, compassion, empathy, and love.

> *Grace is divine empowerment: to live a godly life that is specifically designed to be impossible apart from Christ!*

Grace is divine empowerment: to live a godly life that is specifically *designed* to be *impossible* apart from Christ!

PERSONAL REFLECTION AND PRACTICAL APPLICATION

Honestly ask yourself and the Holy Spirit if there are any areas of your life or business in which you could benefit from a deeper revelation of God's grace for divine empowerment. It could be a business problem that seems insurmountable, an addiction, health, finances, unforgiveness, etc. Grace will _never_ condemn you; nor will it leave you permanently stuck in sin or dysfunction. 1 Corinthians 15:10 assures us that God's grace gets results, but like Paul, you'll find that "...it was not I but *God* who was working *through* me by his grace." If you do feel stuck, don't stop halfway; swim down to the depths of God's grace where you will receive life-giving oxygen for your body and soul. Grace gives you divine empowerment!

CHAPTER 21

GRACE-BASED GIVING

Building on the revelation that God's grace gives us divine empowerment for godly living, let's now apply that to the power of financial giving. This is another one of those paradoxical truths about God's Kingdom: The more you give, the more you receive. It's kind of like the truth that "you must lose your life in order to save it," "the first shall be last and the last shall be first," and, of course, the one that most astonishes me personally: God's Best = *Less* Stress + *More* Rest + *Greater* Success.

For much of my Christian life, I dutifully and obediently gave my tithe to the Lord. I was always taught that's what I'm supposed to do as a good Christian to prove my faithfulness and receive (read *"earn"*) God's blessing. For those who may not be familiar, a "tithe" means a "tenth," which is the percentage of our income that most churches teach we are obligated to give God. Typically, this 10% of our income is given to a local church, charity, missions trips, ministries, etc.

There are many fear-based teachings that use the well-known Old Testament curse found in Malachi 3:8–9 (NASB, my emphasis): "Will a man rob God? Yet you are robbing Me! But you say, 'How have we robbed you?' In tithes and offerings. **You**

215

are cursed with a curse, for you are robbing Me, the whole nation of you!'" The flip side of this is contained in the verses which follow (Malachi 3:10–12 NASB):

> Bring the whole tithe into the storehouse, so that there may be food in My house, and test Me now in this," says the Lord of hosts, "if I will not open for you the windows of heaven and pour out for you a blessing until it overflows. Then I will rebuke the devourer for you, so that it will not destroy the fruits of the ground; nor will your vine in the field cast its grapes," says the Lord of hosts. "All the nations will call you blessed, for you shall be a delightful land," says the Lord of hosts.

This is quintessential Old Covenant law, which uses "carrots and sticks:" punishment for bad behavior and blessing for good behavior. Do bad, get bad; do good, get good. The fundamental premise is based on *us*. We will be rewarded or punished based on what *we* do or don't do. It sounds good, just, and fair. It makes sense to our human minds, and it does contain elements of truth and goodness. But this legalistic system of human-centered behavior and outcomes has been **abolished and replaced** by a New (and *better*) Covenant (Hebrews 8:6–13 NLT, my emphasis):

> But now Jesus, our High Priest, has been given a ministry that is far superior to the old priesthood, for he is the one who mediates for us a far **better** covenant with God, based on **better** promises... When **God** speaks of a "new" covenant, it means **he** has made the first one obsolete...

Notice that *God* did away with the Old Covenant and replaced it with the New Covenant. He did this not because of any fault with the law (which is perfect, holy, and just) but of man's inability to remain faithful to the Old Covenant. **The law** is good and necessary *to the extent* that it brings us to the end of ourselves and into Christ, who is Himself the fulfillment of the law. Having perfectly satisfied the requirements of the law, He now has the authority to be the Mediator between God and man of this better covenant, with its better promises.

The New Covenant's promises are better because they give us access to the unmerited favor of God based on the righteousness and perfection of **Jesus**; not ourselves. 2 Corinthians 5:21 (NASB) says, "He made Him [Christ] who knew no sin to be sin on our behalf, so that we might become the righteousness of God in Him." We essentially get an unlimited "line of credit" from Heaven based on the "prequalification letter" Jesus negotiated for us with God the Father. And this is an all-inclusive contract. There are no hidden loopholes in the fine print; it leaves nothing out. It is the basis for our salvation, eternal security, health, deliverance, freedom, and prosperity—everything we will ever need in this life and the next.

This brings us back to the outdated and pervasively misunderstood issue of tithing. Our finances are *not* blessed by God because of if, when, or how much we give back to Him. That curse for not tithing in Malachi no longer applies because Jesus has redeemed us from the curse of the law: "**But Christ has rescued us from the curse pronounced by the law.** When he was hung on the cross, he took upon himself the curse for our wrongdoing. For it is written in the Scriptures, 'Cursed is everyone who is hung on a tree'" (Galatians 3:13 NLT). The "tree" referred to here is the cross Jesus died on.

But it gets even better! Even though we *don't* get punished for *not* tithing, we *do* get rewarded if we *do* tithe! It's like "tails, you don't lose; heads, you win," all of the upside and none of the downside. If it sounds too good to be true, it should! That's what the true Gospel of Grace is all about: the "almost-too-good-to-be-true news" of Jesus' finished work. Something Andrew

Wommack says that I really resonate with is that "you're better off giving 5% or even 1% by faith than 10% or more under the law." Don't forget that grace is more than just not getting the bad things we deserve or getting the good things we don't deserve. Grace gives us divine empowerment and a changed heart to "live better accidentally under grace than you ever did on purpose under the law" (as Andrew also says).

As a perfect example of this, Andrew shared a testimony about one of the senior leaders of his ministry named Joe. Joe had been consistently giving 10% of his income for years, tracking it literally down to the penny! Despite having a fairly well-paying job, he was getting frustrated because he didn't feel that he was prospering after a long period of obedient tithing, and things were getting even worse for him and his family financially.

"You're better off giving 5% or even 1% by faith than 10% or more under the law."

He had a sincere desire to be faithful and honor God in his finances, but he was giving under the legalistic Malachi 3 mindset. He wanted to make sure he didn't get cursed, and that he was proving himself worthy of *earning* God's financial blessing. What it comes down to is that he wasn't giving in faith but rather out of fear and obligation. There was no joy or expectancy in his giving; it was all drudgery and growing frustration. Perhaps he was even resentful toward God for not fulfilling His end of their "deal."

Andrew suggested to Joe that he stop tracking every check and tithe down to the penny so he could perfectly hit the 10% mark. Instead, Andrew encouraged him to give solely on the basis of heartfelt joy and desire to be a blessing and manifest God's love to people and organizations he gave to when, and only when, he felt a prompting in his heart. After a year of doing this without tracking any of his giving, Joe's bank account was significantly more flush with cash than it had been for as long as he could remember. He felt bad, assuming it could only be explained from having given much less generously during the past year than he had in previous years.

He checked his tax return and all of his financial records, only to discover that he had given **24%** over the past year! This was almost *two and a half times* what he had been giving before, yet somehow, he was significantly better off financially. He couldn't believe it; the math he had previously depended on simply didn't add up. And the best part was that he experienced more genuine joy in his heart from giving during that time than he ever had in his life!

This is such an inspiring testimony of how giving under the New Covenant of Grace is such a blessing to both the giver as well as the receiver. It also contrasts the stark difference between Old Covenant religious obligation and demands with New Covenant empowerment and freedom to do the same thing but with a different heart attitude. And clearly, much better results! The Apostle Paul understood this well and gives us the following exhortation: **"Let giving flow from your heart, not from a sense of religious duty. Let it spring up freely from the joy of giving**—all because God loves hilarious generosity! Yes, God is more than ready to overwhelm you with every form of grace, so that you will have more than enough of everything—every moment and in every way. He will make you overflow with abundance in every good thing you do" (2 Corinthians 9:7–8 TPT).

When I got a revelation of this kind of grace-based giving and financial stewardship, I experienced a similar breakthrough. Every week at Charis, we had "chapel" for an hour, where Andrew shared exclusively on biblical finances. He encouraged us to "give where we're fed;" that is, sowing our financial tithes and offerings into whoever and whatever was truly life-giving to us personally, by which we are encouraged and edified. He also said to "sow where you wanna go," meaning to financially support people and organizations who are doing what God had put in my own heart and are currently where I want to be in the future. I knew I was called to writing, speaking, coaching, teaching, and counseling in a business and ministry context. Therefore, I was very intentional and systematic about giving to ministries and people that helped people apply the truth of God's Word and His grace in practical ways.

Some of them were helping people build wealth for Kingdom purposes and in Kingdom ways, some ministered to couples and singles about godly relationships, and some had well-established podcasts. Many of them were operating in the same anointing I felt God has given me and were collectively well-established in writing, speaking, coaching, teaching, and counseling in business and ministry. By God's grace (divine empowerment and provision), for a period of time, **I was giving away more than 50% of my net income**—without even having a job! As Charis Bible College instructor Barry Bennett says, "Faith pays its bills!"

I didn't have to plunge myself into abject poverty to do it. I always had more than enough to cover my basic needs, and I was living a very comfortable and generally enjoyable life. That has actually been the case over the last 10 years or so, during which time I've been able to give tithes, love offerings, and various other financial support at an amount that is truly staggering when I think back and add it all up. And during that time, my net worth easily more than *doubled!* Again, I don't share this to brag, but I feel I'd be remiss in not sharing with you what I believe to be one of the reasons I've been so extravagantly blessed.

However, I should explain that I am naturally wired to be frugal. Because I am single, I am able—and have chosen—to share a nice home with several other guys, so my housing costs are relatively low. My Bible school tuition was completely

> *Those who live to bless others will have blessings heaped upon them.*

paid for by the GI Bill for two of my three years, and it provided me a stipend for living expenses. I choose to drive a 2006 car that has long been paid off, and I don't spend a lot of money on new clothes, eating out at restaurants, or material possessions. I'm not necessarily against any of those things; they simply don't appeal to me as much as they may to other people. As I've mentioned before, I am a minimalist by nature and personally value my time, freedom, and experiences more highly than many other things.

Like Joe, if I really think about it, the numbers seem impossible. But I've found what Proverbs says to be true: "Generosity brings prosperity, but withholding from charity brings poverty. Those who live to bless others will have blessings heaped upon them, and the one who pours out his life to pour out blessings will be saturated with favor" (11:24–25 TPT). As Andrew Wommack says about money, "If God can get it *through* you, He'll get it *to* you."

PERSONAL REFLECTION AND PRACTICAL APPLICATION

Like Joe, have you been tithing legalistically or transactionally as a burdensome duty or requirement to qualify for God's blessing? Are you frustrated due to financial lack, despite having consistently given for a long time? Like Andrew Wommack says, "You're better off giving 1% in faith than 10% under the law." Ask the Holy Spirit for a revelation of a *better* way to give. Meditate on 2 Corinthians 9:7–8 (TPT): "Let giving flow from your heart, not from a sense of religious duty. Let it spring up freely from the joy of giving... God is more than ready to overwhelm you with every form of grace, so that you will have more than enough of everything—every moment and in every way. He will make you overflow with abundance in every good thing you do."

CHAPTER 22

SUPERNATURAL STEWARDSHIP

I'm hoping and praying the last chapter has given you a grace-based perspective on finances. I started a more in-depth discussion of finances with that topic because giving is a foundational habit pattern for godly prosperity, primarily due to the heart attitude that Spirit-led, grace-based giving cultivates. Another aspect to God's grace over our finances is the ability to prosper and be Holy Spirit-led in our business and investment decisions. I refer to this as "supernatural stewardship," a way in which God has greatly blessed me.

I have self-managed my investment and retirement accounts since I first started investing. Over the past 10 years, I've received an overall compound annual growth rate of almost 9% for my non-real estate portfolio. (I'll go into more detail on much higher returns for my real estate investment later in this chapter.) That may not sound like much, but the magic of compound interest has caused that portfolio to nearly *triple* during that time (which included the financial crisis, or Great

Recession.) Of note, these returns were generated by following what is possibly the easiest and most simple long-term strategy imaginable. (<u>Less</u> stress. <u>More</u> rest. *Greater* success.)

From my previous mistake in buying that condo in San Diego, I learned the value of "cashflow:" A property's generation of sufficient income to offset or exceed its expenses on a monthly basis. With enough cashflow, you can afford to hold on to a property—or any other asset—regardless of fluctuations in the overall market or specific asset price. This helps "weather the storm" during periods of economic volatility.

> *These returns were generated by following what is possibly the easiest and most simple long-term strategy imaginable.*

When I bought the fourplex in Ohio, I was looking at it strictly from a cashflow perspective. I was only interested in passive monthly income I could use to live on, and I assumed for planning purposes there would be zero appreciation. I also assumed this would be a long-time "buy-and-hold" property, meaning that I wouldn't sell it. The cashflow was good, and I was able to buy it without using any debt, so I had no reason or desire to sell it.

The interesting thing I learned about properties with high cashflow is that they are very desirable to other investors who are also looking for high-cashflow properties to add to their portfolios. I also just happened to buy it at the perfect time. Of course, I don't believe that was a coincidence at all but rather God's perfect timing. This also relates to what we talked about regarding divine appointments and kairos or "God-opportune moments" that He sets up on our behalf, completely unbeknownst to us.

Even though I wasn't planning to sell it, a few months ago, I was having my monthly call with my property manager, who's also the realtor who sold me the property. She mentioned it seemed to be a really great seller's market right now. Just for grins, I had her pull some "comps" (sales prices of comparable properties that recently sold). She emailed me 10 minutes later after checking the comps, saying, "Now IS the time to sell." Since I had one vacant unit that had recently undergone a fairly significant rehab, it was perfectly "show-ready" for prospective buyers. My realtor told me that's the perfect setup for a listing, as show-ready vacant units typically accelerate the sales timeline by 75%.

We listed it and recently sold it for $175,000, resulting in the following returns (presented on a "net" basis, meaning after all fees have been deducted):

- Internal Rate of Return (IRR): 18%
- Net Present Value (NPV): $54,000
- 2.5-Year Total Return On Invested Capital: 43%

Most importantly, these returns are **non-leveraged** (meaning **no debt of any kind** was used to generate them). In today's economic environment, many experienced real estate syndicators and private equity firms are looked upon favorably by their investor clients for achieving IRR of 8 to 12% and Total Return on Invested Capital of 20 to 25% over a time horizon of three to five years, using a large amount of debt. As a "newbie" individual investor following a strategy that most experienced real estate investors would (justifiably) say is foolish, the Holy Spirit helped me to generate higher returns, in less time, with zero debt! The foolishness of God truly is wiser than human wisdom.

God wants us to trust Him completely in every area of our lives, and He knows that money can get a grip on our hearts as a source of fear and/or greed. He longs for us to trust Him with our finances so we can be free of those negative influences by experiencing His faithfulness and provision, though it can make us uncomfortable. This is why God gave us the Holy Spirit as our Comforter and Guide. The more times we see Him do what seems impossible to us, the deeper and stronger our trust and intimacy with Him becomes.

A common misconception, based on a misquotation of a well-known scripture, is that "money is the root of all evil." That's simply not true. Money is morally neutral; neither good nor evil. It is simply a tool, no different than a hammer. It can be used to either build and bless or tear down and harm. The heart, mind, motivations, and belief system of the *person* who uses money determines whether it is used for good or evil purposes. The verse in question actually says, "For the **love** of money is a root of all kinds of evil, for which some have strayed from the faith in their greediness, and pierced themselves through with many sorrows" (1 Timothy 6:10 NKJV, my emphasis).

God is not at all opposed to us having material possessions, wealth, or money—and lots of it! But He is *very* much opposed to money having *us*. By this, I mean money having such influence over us that we idolize it and look to it as our source instead of God, allowing the desire for riches to corrupt our souls and hurt people in our quest to obtain it. **"Money is *attracted*, not pursued,"** according to motivational speaker Jim Rohn. In

> *In the world, people chase after money and success. In the Kingdom of God, money and success chase after us.*

the world, people chase after money and success. In the Kingdom of God, money and success chase after *us*. Deuteronomy 28:2 says, "And all these blessings shall come upon you and overtake you, because you obey the voice of the Lord your God." When we exercise our faith by resting in God, He will work for us.

God provides for us in ways that increase our trust in Him. When our perspective is clear and our hearts are humble that *He* is our Source, He actually gives us His supernatural power to prosper financially. He does this to bless us, bless others through us, fulfill His promises, and establish His covenant. In much the same way that physical healing is said to be "the dinner bell for salvation," financial prosperity can be a powerful witness of God's goodness that draws people to us and causes them to ask us questions that will have Jesus as the only possible answer.

To this end, Jesus actually instructs us to be cunning, as well as generous. "Pay attention, now! I am sending you out like sheep among wolves. So be as cunning as serpents and as innocent as doves" (Matthew 10:16 ISV). This is said in the context of sending out His disciples to minister in His name, but He could just as well be talking about doing business! He does not want us to be naïve and easily taken advantage of in our business and financial affairs, something He warns against specifically for His followers. Jesus wants us to be shrewd, faithful, and generous representatives of Him in how we handle money and conduct ourselves on this earth for eternal impact, as He describes in Luke 16:8-9 (TPT, my emphasis):

> Jesus continued, "Remember this: The sons of darkness are more shrewd than the sons of light in their interactions with others. **It is important that you use the wealth of this world to demonstrate your friendship with God by winning friends and blessing others.** Then, when this world fails and falls apart, your generosity will provide you with an eternal reward.

Hopefully by now you see that God is not against us being wealthy and prosperous and that money is a powerful tool He has given us to maximize our earthly influence for eternal impact for His Kingdom. The key is in recognizing the *Lord* as our Source for everything we have and stewarding our God-given resources for the betterment of our neighbors, ourselves, and His name throughout the earth. When we approach it from that perspective, He "delights in our prosperity" (Psalms 35:27) and divinely empowers us with *more* than enough for our basic needs so that we can bless others and also be blessed ourselves. There will be times we find ourselves needing it and being blessed by it, but God's grace to endure hardship isn't ultimately His highest or best for us.

Contrary to what some say and may even believe, it is not a badge of honor or more "spiritual" to be broke, poor, sick, or suffering. How is that appealing or winsome to the people we're trying to reach? Why would they want what we have in Jesus if that's what our lives look like? As God's children, it stands to reason that we are the most effective witnesses and ambassadors to the world of His goodness by being the most blessed, prosperous, healthy, and whole people on the earth! When Jesus is clearly at the center of our lives, these blessings will inevitably point to Him. We are called to be both messengers *and* demonstrators of the *Good News Gospel.*

> *The key is in recognizing the Lord as our Source for everything we have.*

PERSONAL REFLECTION AND PRACTICAL APPLICATION

Think and talk to God about whether you have any false narratives or beliefs about God's will for you regarding your finances. This could apply to the mentality you have about giving, being wealthy, money, or how you're stewarding other resources. God has divine purposes for using money and wealth as a tool for expanding God's Kingdom. As Jesus says in Luke 16:9, "It is important that you use the wealth of this world to demonstrate your friendship with God by winning friends and blessing others." Ask the Holy Spirit to lead you to give, save, invest, and use your God-given resources in a way that cannot help but point people to the Good News of Jesus.

CHAPTER 23

WHAT MAKES
YOU COME ALIVE?

In this final chapter, I want to connect the dots of some of the things I've shared up to this point with one of the most profound and life-giving revelations I've received from the Holy Spirit. In the last chapter, we talked about how being Spirit-led will result in supernatural stewardship and God-given prosperity. In Luke 16, Jesus said it was important to use the wealth of this world for eternal reasons.

*This highest form of stewardship starts with yourself: mining and stewarding the riches the Lord has put inside you in the form of your God-given personality, gifts, passions, talents, and **divine purpose.***

However, Jesus considered money as "least" in the Kingdom of God, and referred to it as a training tool in character development for being entrusted with the "true riches." I've heard teachings that the "true riches" Jesus referred to are *people*. Being that people are eternal (in their spirit) and that God paid the highest possible price for people (with Jesus), stewardship of people is of the highest importance to God.

I agree, and I'd like to suggest that this highest form of stewardship starts with *yourself*: mining and stewarding the riches the Lord has put inside you in the form of your God-given personality, gifts, passions, talents, and **divine purpose**. God has lovingly created and personally designed you in a very specific way that is purposefully aligned with your God-given calling. In Psalms 139:13–14 (NIV), David says to the Lord, "For you created my inmost being; you knit me together in my mother's womb. I praise you because I am fearfully and wonderfully made; your works are wonderful, I know that full well." We are each beautifully hand-crafted masterpieces of our Heavenly Father, uniquely designed for fulfillment and effectiveness. We are not designed to be frustrated and burned out in life!

As part of my own journey of investigation into identifying and living out my divine purpose, I read a book called *StrengthsFinder 2.0* by Tom Rath. *StrengthsFinder* was based on a large body of research conducted by the Gallup organization. The research led them to the conclusion that most people are far better served by focusing primarily on using their natural strengths instead of attempting to overcome their weaknesses. This is the main philosophy of the book, which gave me a life-giving and life-changing paradigm shift.

The author used an illustration based on the life of Rudy Ruettiger, popularized by the movie *Rudy*. American culture has celebrated this story about a man who had "not one lick of natural talent" but through sheer grit and determination overcame his weaknesses to achieve his dream of playing Notre Dame football. Going against the tide of popular opinion, the book identified Rudy as an example to be avoided rather than aspired to. The reasoning the author simply and powerfully laid out was that if Rudy had applied the same level of focus and intensity in the area of his greatest *natural* strength, he would have achieved a much higher return on investment for his life's efforts, including greater fulfillment.

Furthermore, the research indicates that everyone has within them a certain number of natural strengths. When intentionally developed and frequently used, these strengths produce significantly greater professional productivity and deeper personal fulfillment. The possibility of this idea absolutely fascinated me. As one who was familiar with toiling and fighting an uphill battle against the grain and feeling like a round peg in a square hole at times, this gave me an incredible sense of hope and inspiration. Up until this time, I had always believed that if you wanted to get a "good job" you were just going to have to suck it up. If it was enjoyable work, they wouldn't have to pay you to do it, right?

> *"Don't ask what the world needs. Ask what makes you come alive, and go do it. Because what the world needs is people who have come alive."*

Wrong. According to the book's research, those who focus on operating within their strengths are not only more productive and fulfilled in what they do, they are also the most highly compensated. This makes sense when you think about it because people are ultimately compensated based on the value they provide, not their job title or the number of hours they work. People who are truly passionate about and naturally gifted in their work generally add more value for those they're serving.

I want to repeat a previously used quote from educator and civil rights activist Howard Thurman: "Don't ask what the world needs. Ask what makes you come alive, and go do it. Because what the world needs is people who have come alive." This is what Jesus came to give and what the world so desperately needs: for us to be fully alive! I want to capture the richness of this by using several different translations of John 10:10, in which Jesus says, "I came so they can have real and eternal life, more and better life than they ever dreamed of" (MSG). "But I have come to give you everything in abundance, more than you expect—life in its fullness until you overflow!" (TPT). "I came that they may have and enjoy life…" (AMPC). "My purpose is to give them a rich and satisfying life" (NLT).

> *The sweet spot is where you experience your deepest fulfillment and greatest effectiveness in serving others.*

Thurman's quote and John 10:10 are some of the pieces to a puzzle the Holy Spirit has been helping me put together for almost a decade now. This has resulted in the profound and life-giving revelation of something I call the "sweet spot." The sweet spot is where you experience your deepest fulfillment and greatest effectiveness in serving others. It's also where you will receive your greatest "compensation:" professionally, financially, emotionally, spiritually, and relationally. When you're in your sweet spot, you'll be well-paid to do what you love most and do best! From an engineering perspective, think of it as the optimal parameters for your unique God-given design specifications in service of your divine purpose.

The sweet spot is the intersection of four things: your deepest passion, your deepest pain, your greatest strength, and your greatest service. You can visualize these four things as overlapping circles, somewhat like a Venn Diagram, with the sweet spot in the center. Included is a defining graphic that sums it up visually.

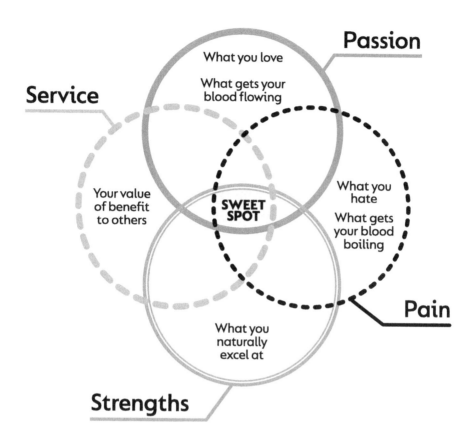

If you play tennis, you're probably familiar with the sweet spot. When you hit a tennis ball within the sweet spot of a tennis racquet, you get optimal power, accuracy, and effectiveness. It's where you can smoothly and almost effortlessly hit your best shots. I came across this description of the sweet spot while doing some online research: "If a ball impacts at the sweet spot, the force transmitted to the hand is sufficiently small that the player is **almost unaware that the impact has occurred**" (my emphasis). This gives us *greater* **effectiveness** with *less* **effort**. This relationship between minimal effort and optimal outcome confirms to me that "God's Best = Less Stress + More Rest + <u>Greater</u> Success".

When I say "minimal effort and optimal outcome," please don't misunderstand me. Hitting the sweet spot does not happen automatically or effortlessly *at first*. It's similar to "laboring to enter into rest." In tennis, it requires a high degree of focus, time, and intentionality to consistently hit the ball in the sweet spot of the racquet. With patience and persistence, though, it will eventually become smooth and effortless.

Assuming you really like playing tennis and are athletically inclined to do so, this process will be more enjoyable than frustrating. Similarly in life, I've been on a ten-year journey investigating and refining my own sweet spot. I still haven't fully arrived, and in some ways, I'm actually just getting started. But it's generally been an enjoyable and enriching process for me along the way.

Even when hitting our sweet spot is automatic and effortless from the start, that has its own challenges. In life as well as in tennis, when we're hitting in our sweet spot, it can be so natural and effortless that we sometimes don't even realize our "impact." For example, throughout my life, people have opened up to me and shared things they rarely, if ever, share with anyone; even people I barely know.

This happened without my conscious awareness for a long time until only several years ago when the Holy Spirit highlighted to me that I have a gift of empathic listening and counseling. Without any effort or intentionality, people feel safe opening up to me and naturally seeking my counsel or advice. Now that I'm finally aware of my "impact," this is a natural strength that I intentionally leverage to add more value to people around me, a process by which I'm also more personally fulfilled and effective.

Conversely, "If the ball impacts at a point well away from the sweet spot, the player will feel some jarring and vibration of the handle." Both in tennis and life, this "missing" of the sweet spot results in more pain, less power, and less accuracy. This territory

236

is where we hit our worst shots: **more effort, greater pain,** and **less effectiveness.** The bottom line here is to focus the majority of your time identifying, enlarging, and consistently hitting *in* your sweet spot instead of outside it. How do we do that?

The Pareto Principle, or 80/20 Rule, gives us some insight. Consistently, studies have shown that 80% of our results or output are provided by 20% of our input. In business, this usually means that 20% of your clients will give you 80% of your revenue and/or referrals. From a StrengthsFinder approach, approximately the top 20% of your strengths result in 80% of your productivity and fulfillment. (The reverse is also true: 20% of your business clients or employees will cause you 80% of your headaches.) Therefore, the key is to **focus on the 20% of your inputs that generate 80% of your positive results.**

Focusing on the 80% of your least natural and effective personal strengths is a far less wise and effective use of your time and energy than focusing the majority of your time on your top 20% strengths. It will also require more effort and be more painful. This concept applies to every area of life: spiritual gifts, business, relationships, management, employment, and the list goes on. If you have a gift of encouragement, don't spend most of your time trying to shore up your weaknesses by serving as an administrator or in the ministry of helps. If you're a big-picture visionary, don't try to micromanage the details of the business. **Accept how God uniquely made you; don't frustrate yourself (or others!) by trying to be something or someone you're not.**

I want to make another important caveat: I'm not saying there isn't ever a need to overcome personal weaknesses or cultivate personal growth by only and always doing what comes easily and naturally. In fact, personal growth is at the very heart of this message. As I hope you've seen through my story, God's grace has helped me grow and stretch in ways I never would have imagined.

In some ways, your God-given calling may be *despite* your natural inclinations, as opposed to because of them. Andrew Wommack shared that he was so painfully shy and introverted, he couldn't even look people in the face to say hi. He couldn't have imagined a vocation as a public speaker, yet now he speaks regularly in front of thousands of people and is broadcast on TV to billions around the globe. I'm naturally very analytical, performance-oriented, and legalistically inclined. Yet my life message is about God's grace and rest, and I've made a number of very illogical choices about major life decisions.

But it's also true that Andrew is a naturally brilliant teacher and minister of the Gospel, who genuinely loves studying and teaching the Word of God. I've always been a natural communicator and analytical money manager with a passion for connecting with and inspiring people. So it's both/and: God *will* use your passions and desires, *and* He'll do it in a way you would never have expected through a process that brings you way out of your own abilities so you learn to depend on Him. More than anything, though, it will be so much **better** than what you would have envisioned or been able to do on your own.

When you've identified and started operating within your own sweet spot, it's easier to help other people identify and operate within their own. By using your accumulated wisdom and experience, you will more easily be able to identify another person's latent gift or talent they're not consciously aware of and help them cultivate it. The opposite is also true: You may be able to offer perspective and advice from dealing with your own frustrations and struggles to help someone realize they're operating outside their own sweet spot. This allows you to be an even more effective steward of the "true riches" in other people on whom you can have a potentially life-changing and eternal impact.

This truth is even more powerful in a corporate (group) environment, whether that's a family, church, business, etc. The beautiful thing about the way God designed us is that we work synergistically together, where the whole is greater than the sum of the parts. God created us for healthy interdependence on Him and each other to accomplish the purposes He created us for. Where you're weak, someone else is strong and vice versa. We see this demonstrated in economist David Ricardo's concept of "specialization:" countries will specialize in making the goods they can produce most efficiently—their areas of comparative advantage—and trade for goods they make less well, rather than making all kinds of products for themselves.

The result is higher output/productivity both individually and collectively. In other words, we can expand the overall pie as well as each slice within it. This makes everyone better off. When we identify and specialize in our personal areas of "comparative advantage" within the Body of Christ (to include business or any other field), it's like a hand in a glove—a perfect fit for the mutual and maximum benefit of all. Ephesians 4:16 (NLT) says, "He makes the whole body fit together perfectly. As each part does its own special work, it helps the other parts grow, so that the whole body is healthy and growing and full of love." How wonderful that is! You get to be you, I get to be me, and we all get blessed, not only in receiving, but even more so in giving.

Ephesians 2:10 (TLB) says, "It is God himself who has made us what we are and given us new lives from Christ Jesus; and long ages ago he planned that we should spend these lives in helping others." I used to think of service and spending my life helping others as a burdensome duty I needed to fulfill in order to be a good person and a faithful follower of Christ. But this all changed when I got this revelation about the sweet spot! I realized it's our uniquely life-giving contribution to the world:

life-giving not only for those you're benefiting and serving, but also life-giving to you in the very act of providing that service.

Philippians 2:13 (AMPC, my emphasis) is another verse that has changed my life and my thinking: "[**Not in your own strength**] for it is *God* Who is all the while effectually at work in you [**energizing** and creating in you the power **and desire**], both to will and to work for His good pleasure and satisfaction and delight." It almost sounds too good to be true… you and I not only get blessed by others, but we also get blessed in the very act of blessing them. And *God* is the One who's energizing the whole process to give us both the energy *and* the desire to do it. Whereas I used to think of doing God's will as a difficult and demanding requirement of Christian service, this revelation now makes the idea of serving God and serving people something I'm genuinely passionate about and thankful for!

A personal testimony about this was the capstone project at Charis Business School during my third year. This capstone project involves putting together a business pitch for an entrepreneurial idea, which is presented to a panel of business experts. Every student pitches their own idea, and the panel selects a small number of ideas to put a student team around to further develop a business plan. I was put on a team supporting and developing another person's idea, which I wasn't all that excited about. The combination of disappointment from my pitch not being selected along with the lack of enthusiasm about the project idea I was now assigned to made it difficult to engage wholeheartedly in this project.

As I was talking to God about this, I sensed Him tell me to resolve within myself to commit my mind and heart to the process with this team I was assigned to. I sensed Him say to me that if I would work on this with the highest levels of excellence, working as unto Him with a great heart attitude about it, that this would open doors of opportunity. It was hard at first, and our group ran into many roadblocks and had to pivot from the original idea multiple times.

Eventually, though, this project morphed into a real estate investment idea for which I was able to apply my personal interest and experience. Once I started running the numbers on these properties, I got excited. This was no longer just a mandatory school assignment to complete but something I truly and passionately threw myself into! I spent countless hours on this project, going above and beyond what was expected or required, but since I was working in my sweet spot, it didn't feel like work.

Like Paul said in 1 Corinthians 15:10 (MSG), "It was God giving me the work to do, God giving me the energy to do it." As the saying goes, "If you love what you do, you never work a day in your life." This is the reason I am so intentional about building passive income. The goal of passive income is not to *stop* working; it's to have the financial freedom to throw yourself wholeheartedly into work that you truly love and WANT to do! Again, God has given us work as a *blessing*!

After Adam and Eve sinned, God said, "Cursed is the ground for your sake; in **toil** you shall eat of it all the days of your life. Both thorns and thistles it shall bring forth for you… In the sweat of your face you shall eat bread…" (Genesis 3:17–19 NKJV, my emphasis). This cursed toil is what I refer to as "*hard*

> *The goal of passive income is not to stop working; it's to have the financial freedom to throw yourself wholeheartedly into work that you truly love and WANT to do!*

work." Proverbs 10:22 says, "The blessing of the Lord—it makes **[truly]** rich, and He adds **no sorrow with it [neither does toiling increase it]**" (AMPC, my emphasis). I say "hard work is ungodly" because God gives us fulfilling and meaningful work that we're designed to enjoy and be *truly* enriched by.

As I was working on this project, a friend of mine I hadn't talked to for almost a year called me out of the blue to talk about real estate investing. He knew nothing about this project I was working on, but it led to a series of discussions with another very experienced and successful real estate investor I'd met several years before. Our conversations provided a depth of insight that was brought to bear on this school project. As a result, the final presentation went so well that I was asked to teach and coach business students as an adjunct professor at Charis Business School!

> *I say "hard work is ungodly" because God gives us fulfilling and meaningful work that we're designed to enjoy and be truly enriched by.*

This opportunity perfectly aligns with the calling I received from God in Vail right after my snowboarding accident in 2016. At that time, I felt a deep knowing that I am called to writing, speaking, teaching, coaching, and counseling in business and ministry. And even though we didn't pursue this specific school project, I am now still talking to these two outside investors about other deals as well as a possible longer-term partnership. I believe this could lead to opportunities I've recently been praying for that are an *ideal* fit for my sweet spot.

There's no doubt in my mind that this timely connection with these two investors and my teaching and coaching opportunity at Charis are God-ordained divine appointments. I had absolutely no input on being assigned to the group project that I was. This project transformed from a burdensome task to an exciting opportunity. As I trusted and submitted to Him, God divinely empowered me for this assignment and put me right in my sweet spot. Once again, what started as a disappointment and looked like a setback was actually a setup for divine appointments and

Finding your sweet spot will fill you to overflowing with hope, passion, excellence, service, and gratitude!

kairos moments for opportunities that align with my calling. It has all happened like God said that it would but in ways that I never would have imagined.

Part of investing in rest for God's best is taking the time and being intentional to mine the riches He's placed inside you to be used for your benefit and the benefit of others. Proverbs 25:2 tells us this: "God conceals the revelation of his word in the hiding place of his glory. But the honor of kings is revealed by how they thoroughly search out the deeper meaning of all that God says." Part of the revelation of God's Word that we have the privilege of thoroughly searching out is about ourselves. Having been on this journey for many years, I can say it's a stimulating and edifying process of discovery that we have the blessing of engaging in with God and each other. Finding your sweet spot will fill you to overflowing with hope, passion, excellence, service, and gratitude!

PERSONAL REFLECTION AND PRACTICAL APPLICATION

"Don't ask what the world needs. Ask what makes you come alive, and go do it. Because what the world needs is people who have come alive." What makes *you* come alive? Jesus came to give us a fulfilling and abundant life (John 10:10). Have you identified your "sweet spot," and are you operating in it? Invest time discovering how your unique, God-given personality and gifts are designed to bring you life by serving others. Meditate on Philippians 2:13: "[Not in your own strength] for it is *God* Who is all the while effectually at work in you [energizing and creating in you the power and desire], both to will and to work for His good pleasure and satisfaction and delight." Part of God's *best* for us is to manifest His goodness by being fully alive and deeply fulfilled in living out the purpose and calling He's given us by blessing and serving others!

CONCLUSION

What a journey! From crashing a helicopter and going from the lowest point of my life to experiencing the "divine trampoline" of going from setback to setup multiple times since then. I've shared with you a lot about my personal struggles with anxiety and deep lack of fulfillment in my work. We've gone on a journey of discovery, becoming increasingly aware that God has a far better way and plan for our lives than anything the world can offer. In wholeheartedly seeking after God's best, we've embarked on many scary and exciting Spirit-led adventures of walking by faith that resulted in several major life transitions.

Through these experiences, we've experienced both the spirituality and *practicality* of entering into God's grace by repenting of self-effort. We've seen first-hand how this "investment in rest" yields God's best for our lives with less stress and *greater* success—a success that has quantitative, bottom-line results as well as qualitative and eternal significance. We've established that grace gives us divine empowerment to live a godly life and that God's best for us is not striving and toiling to be something or someone we're not.

God has a far better way and plan for our lives than anything the world can offer.

Finally, we talked about how being Spirit-led will result in supernatural stewardship and God-given prosperity, which is best exemplified by stewarding the "true riches" the Lord has placed within us and others in the form of our unique God-given design and purpose. We steward these inner riches by identifying our "sweet spot" so we can do what makes us come alive and experience the full and satisfying life Jesus came to give us.

A final word about investing in rest and what that can look like: Sometimes, when opportunities are presented to us, it's good and necessary to give a brief pause to pray and seek the Lord about it. There are times we have to say no to something really good so that we can say yes to something even *better* God has for us. I've recently had to do this, even though it didn't make sense. The willingness and ability to embrace counterintuitive and countercultural Spirit-led thinking will prove that "the foolishness of God is wiser than human wisdom, and the weakness of God is stronger than human strength."

I pray that the personal stories and testimonies I've shared in this book have brought the Word of God to life for you in a new way that has encouraged and challenged your own thinking. Hopefully you can see how the supernatural meets the practical and are inspired to "live a life that *demands* a supernatural explanation." To that end, I have included a number of spiritual and practical resources that have helped me tremendously in my own journey. I encourage you to look at those in the "Resources" section of this book.

I want to end by reiterating that **grace is the whole package, from start to finish. Grace is what sets Christianity apart from every**

> *Sometimes, when opportunities are presented to us, it's good and necessary to give a brief pause to pray and seek the Lord about it.*

other religion. We have the opportunity to enter into God's rest and blessing based solely on the finished work of Jesus. This is the too-good-to-be-true news of the Gospel! Regardless of where you are in your personal journey and faith, more than anything, I hope that you have had a life-changing revelation of God's goodness. Theologian and author A. W. Tozer said, "What comes into our minds when we think about God is the most important thing about us... the most portentous fact about any man is not what he at a given time may say or do, but what he in his deep heart conceives God to be like."

I can tell you from my own personal experience that a revelation in my deep heart of God's goodness has transformed my life for the better in every way. "Never doubt God's mighty power to work in you and accomplish all this. He will achieve infinitely more than your greatest request, your most unbelievable dream, and exceed your wildest imagination! He will outdo them all, for his miraculous power constantly energizes you." (Ephesians 3:20, TPT)

What comes into our minds when we think about God is the most important thing about us...

God's best to you,

RYAN HALEY

Resources

Below are some books and resources that have been especially helpful to me in my personal journey in receiving a revelation of God's grace, as well as doing business and life God's better way. There are also practical resources to help you in your personal and professional development. This is certainly not an all-inclusive list, but a starting point for understanding and practically applying the "almost-too-good-to-be-true-news" of the Gospel.

A Better Way: https://ABetterWayPodcast.com (for general information and to subscribe for email updates)

- **Coaching:** https://abetterwaypodcast.com/coaching
- **Speaking:** https://abetterwaypodcast.com/speaking
- **Blog:** https://abetterwaypodcast.com/blog
- **Podcast:** https://anchor.fm/abetterway
- **Partner:** https://abetterwaypodcast.com/partner
- **Sweet Spot Teaching:** https://abetterwaypodcast.com/sweet-spot

Joseph Prince: https://www.josephprince.com

- *Destined to Reign: The Secret to Effortless Success, Wholeness and Victorious Living*
- *Unmerited Favor: Your Supernatural Advantage for a Successful Life*

Paul Ellis: https://escapetoreality.org

- *The Hyper Grace Gospel: A Response to Michael Brown and Those Opposed to the Modern Grace Message*
- www.KingsPress.org (links to other Paul Ellis books)

Dan Stone and Greg Smith: *The Rest of the Gospel: When the Partial Gospel Has Worn You Out*

Mike Davis, Rocky Mountain Family Church: https://www.rmfchurch.org

Shae Bynes, Kingdom Driven Entrepreneur: https://kingdomdrivenentrepreneur.com

- *Grace Over Grind: How Grace Will Take Your Business Where Grinding Can't*

Steve McVey: https://www.gracewalk.org

- *Grace Walk: What You've Always Wanted in the Christian Life*

Arthur Meintjes, Kingdom Life Ministry: https://arthurmeintjes.com

- *Knowing and Experiencing God*

Jason Clark: www.afamilystory.org

Andy Mason: https://heaveninbusiness.com

- *God With You at Work (Heaven in Business Book 1)*

Blake and Linda Schellenberg, CoLabor Ministries:
https://colaborministries.org

Andrew Wommack: https://www.awmi.net

- *Living in God's Best: Don't Settle for Less*

Sarah Young: *Jesus Calling: Enjoying Peace in His Presence*

Tom Rath, StrengthsFinder:
https://www.gallup.com/cliftonstrengths/en/home.aspx

- *StrengthsFinder 2.0*

Charles R. Wade Jr.: *Designed for Fulfillment: A Study of the Redemptive Gifts*

Robert T. Kiyosaki and Tim Wheeler: *Rich Dad Poor Dad: What the Rich Teach Their Kids About Money That the Poor and Middle Class Do Not!*

BiggerPockets: www.biggerpockets.com

- Real estate investing resources (online community, forums, podcast, tutorials, etc.)

John C. Bogle: *The Little Book of Common Sense Investing: The Only Way to Guarantee Your Fair Share of Stock Market Returns*

Dave Ramsey: https://www.daveramsey.com/fpu

- *Financial Peace: Restoring Financial Hope to You and Your Family*

Dog Tag Fellowship Program:
https://www.dogtaginc.org/fellowship

- Fellowship program for transitioning military members, spouses, and caregivers

Review Inquiry

HEY, IT'S RYAN HALEY HERE.

I hope you've enjoyed the book, finding it both useful and fun. I have a favor to ask you.

Would you consider giving it a rating on Amazon or wherever you bought the book? Online book stores are more likely to promote a book when they feel good about its content, and reader reviews are a great barometer for a book's quality.

So please go to Amazon.com (or wherever you bought the book), search for my name and the book title, and leave a review. If someone gave you a copy of my book, then leave a review on Amazon and maybe consider adding a picture of you holding the book. That increases the likelihood your review will be accepted!

Many thanks in advance,
RYAN HALEY

Will You Share the Love?

GET THIS BOOK FOR A FRIEND, ASSOCIATE OR FAMILY MEMBER!

If you have found this book valuable and know others who would find it useful, consider buying them a copy as a gift. Special bulk discounts are available if you would like your whole team or organization to benefit from reading this.

Just contact Ryan@GodsBetterWay.com.

Would You Like Ryan Haley to Speak at Your Organization?

BOOK RYAN NOW!

Ryan accepts a limited number of speaking, coaching, and training engagements each year. To learn how you can bring his message to your organization,

**visit
https://ABetterWayPodcast.com**

**or email him at
Ryan@GodsBetterWay.com.**

ABOUT THE AUTHOR

 Ryan Haley is a former U.S. Navy Officer, SH-60B helicopter pilot, Afghanistan combat veteran, and Pentagon defense budget analyst. In 2007, a helicopter crash served as a dramatic wake-up call for Ryan to live a purposeful life centered around his faith in God. His life message is about God's grace and the "too-good-to-be-true news" of the Gospel of Jesus. Ryan is called to inspirational communication and personal development as a writer, speaker, coach, teacher, and counselor.

Ryan is the founder of *A Better Way*, a media and teaching platform that inspires people to experience "where the supernatural meets the practical" in faith, business, and life. *A Better Way* currently includes a podcast, blog, website, and book. Ryan's mission is to apply the practicality and power of God's grace in helping people and organizations experience deeper fulfillment and greater effectiveness by tapping into their deepest passions, deepest pain, and greatest strengths to provide maximum service and value to others.

Ryan is an adjunct professor at Charis Bible College Business School, a real estate investor, and self-manager of his retirement and investment portfolio. Ryan has worked as a Pentagon defense budget analyst managing a $4.5 billion annual appropriation, a licensed realtor, and sales and account manager of a tech startup. His extensive educational background is complemented by personal experience in business, entrepreneurship, and financial investing. Ryan's desire is to use his wealth-building acumen and leadership skills in helping others reach financial freedom and empower them to be unhindered in following their God-given dreams and purpose.

Ryan received his MBA in Financial Management from the Naval Postgraduate School, a postgraduate Business Administration certificate from Georgetown University, and his BA in Psychology from the University of San Diego. He also finished a two-year biblical studies program at Charis Bible College in Woodland Park, Colorado, where he received his Christian Ministers License and completed a subsequent third-year business program.

Ryan is originally from Portland, Oregon. He lives in Woodland Park, Colorado, where he enjoys the beauty of the mountains and outdoors through hiking, snowboarding, and playing disc golf. He also enjoys being part of church and small group fellowships.

You can schedule Ryan for speaking and coaching engagements as well as sign up for a free weekly email list through A Better Way's website: **https://ABetterWayPodcast.com.** Ryan's email is **Ryan@GodsBetterWay.com.**

Made in the USA
Middletown, DE
05 November 2020

23389331R00156